Michael O'Donnell

GW00390955

IRISH POLITICAL PARTIES
An Introduction

In the same series:

CHAIRMAN OR CHIEF?: the role of Taoiseach in Irish Government
Brian Farrell

THE FOUNDING OF DÁIL ÉIREANN: Parliament and Nation Building
Brian Farrell

THE IRISH POLITICAL ELITE
Al Cohan

Studies in Irish Political Culture 3

IRISH POLITICAL PARTIES
An Introduction

MAURICE MANNING

GILL AND MACMILLAN

First published in 1972

Gill and Macmillan Limited

2 Belvedere Place

Dublin 1

and in London through association with the
Macmillan
Group of Publishing Companies

7171 0536 9

Cover designed by Graham Shepherd

Printing history:
10 9 8 7 6 5 4 3 2 1

Printed and bound in the Republic of Ireland by
Cahill & Co. Limited Dublin 8

For Marcel and Renée St. Oven

'Party divisions whether on the whole operating for good or evil are things inseparable from free government. This is a truth which I believe admits little dispute, having been established by the uniform experience of all ages.'

Edmund Burke

ACKNOWLEDGEMENTS

I wish to thank Gallup (Ireland) and the Labour party for permission to reproduce some of their tables from their very valuable 1969 survey.

I would like also to thank my colleague Tom Garvin for useful help and comment, the editor of the series Brian Farrell for his consistent help and Miss Avila Kilmurray for some very pertinent suggestions. And as usual Professor Conor Martin could not have been more encouraging or helpful.

A final word of thanks for the ultra-efficient typing services of Miss Elizabeth Sheppard and Miss Mary Furlong.

Maurice Manning
February 1972

Contents

1

Irish Political Parties Before 1922

Had Home Rule become a reality in Southern Ireland prior to 1914, it is virtually certain that the dominant political party in the new state would have been the Home Rule or Parliamentary Party. When however a form of Home Rule was conceded eight years later that party had been all but obliterated, swept away by a movement which was itself to be destroyed in the flames of civil war, but from which was to spring the two political groups which have dominated Irish politics since that day.

Perhaps the most obvious feature of Irish politics in the forty years prior to 1916 was the position of dominance enjoyed by the Home Rule party. This party, founded by Isaac Butt, shaped by Charles Stewart Parnell, had during these years the unchallenged support and unquestioned allegiance of the great majority of nationalist Ireland. Its objective of Home Rule was a majority aspiration and its leaders such as John Redmond and John Dillon were well known and securely established political figures.

True, the party had been seriously and bitterly divided after the Parnell split in 1890 and indeed the years immediately following had been filled with bitterness and incessant internal strife. However, between 1898 and 1900 the party had been re-united under the leadership of the Parnellite John Redmond and under him it had regained much of its stability and some of its earlier drive.

No rival political party had as yet arisen to challenge this supremacy with any real hope of success. Sinn Féin was still small and largely concerned with cultural and economic matters. The Labour party was not formed until 1912 and then made little impact. The only real challenge came in the

Ulster counties where the Home Rule issue took on a particular virulence and where the Unionist party dominated. The differences between the Unionists and the Home Rulers were seen as fundamental and especially in view of the sectarian character of the support given to each party, their sources of support did not overlap. As a result each party had areas of uncontested supremacy—in the December election of 1910 for example more than 50 of the seats won by the Home Rule party were uncontested and the same was true of 11 Unionist seats. The result of this was that many constituencies had not known an electoral contest for more than a decade.

*   *   *

If ever a party appeared invincible the Home Rule party did and this seeming invincibility made all the more dramatic the shock of its annihilation in the general election of 1918. Rarely has so dominant a party disappeared so suddenly and with such little ceremony. In a sense it was not just the Home Rule party but a whole political ethos which was wiped out overnight.

It is clear now that by the 1918 election the Home Rule party was in serious decline. The Parnellite split had never been completely healed with the result that disunity and internal disagreement were always a threat. This in turn meant that the spectacle of the party devoting so much of its time to bitter personal feuds and futile vendettas was likely to lessen its attractiveness to many younger voters. The fact that so many seats were 'safe' seats and the absence of competitiveness generally, induced complacency and lethargy on the part of some members. More seriously the growing intransigence of Unionist resistance to Home Rule and the increasing likelihood of a partition settlement was proving to be a source of great disappointment just when it looked as if Home Rule was about to be attained.

None of these factors on their own was likely to inflict permanent damage on the party—each might have been overcome and the Home Rule leaders taken their place in the government of a Home Rule Ireland had it not been for the series of events triggered off by the 1916 Rising, in particular the emergence of a powerful and popular alternative to the Parliamentary Party. This in fact was to be one of the most lasting legacies of the 1916 Rising—the events which followed it created a climate which made possible the emergence of Sinn Féin as a major political force—and with it the decline of the hitherto unchallengeable Parliamentary Party.

The Sinn Féin party which emerged after 1916 was very different from that of a few years earlier. The party which existed between 1905–1917 would have been satisfied with independence within a dual monarchy system. It was a small party whose infrequent electoral attempts had not been particularly successful and its members were usually more interested in social, cultural and economic nationalism. It was in no sense a mass or popular party. Circumstances after 1916 however brought together in common opposition to British government policy in Ireland such groups as Sinn Féin, the Liberty Clubs, the National League and the released 1916 'Prisoners' Associations', and the composite body which evolved became known as the new or second Sinn Féin party.

This new party spread rapidly during 1917. Sinn Féin clubs were set up throughout the country—growing during 1917 to 1,200 clubs and 25,000 members, winning support from many who had never before been involved in politics and from others whose allegiance had hitherto been to the Home Rule party. Sinn Féin did not develop independently —it was in fact the political wing of a military and political movement and not surprisingly there was considerable overlap between the two sections. As a result of this and indeed as an inevitable product of the uncertainty and instability of the time the new party took shape sometimes in a confused and chaotic manner. Its early days were to know plenty of internal wrangling and quarrelling over points of policy and procedure. Personality and organisational difference almost precipitated a split on two occasions during 1917.[1]

The leaders of Sinn Féin placed the highest possible value on the unity of the movement and on the need to con-

3

centrate all energies and attention on the one issue of fundamental importance—that of independence. Attempts were made to play down potentially divisive issues—even such issues as 'the Republic' and partition were not discussed at any great length. The main preoccupations until the end of the Anglo-Irish war were the down-to-earth questions of staying in existence, of creating a mass movement and of fighting elections. According to one student of the period it was this very 'practical mindedness' which contributed to much of Sinn Féin's success[2]—but it also cloaked the fact that it was never a monolithic and totally united political party but rather a coalition of differing groups held together by their common objective of securing independence and by their common enemy, the British government.

The decisive victory of 1918 meant the dramatic replacement of one political generation by a new one. Many who might not otherwise have entered politics now found themselves elected to parliament, swept in on a tide strong enough to keep them in for a lifetime. Victory also meant a change in emphasis in Sinn Féin policy. Sinn Féin now regarded itself as the legitimate government of the country and its previous emphasis on the building up of a party machine and the winning of elections was now replaced by a determination to supplant in Ireland the whole apparatus of British rule.

Later, with the suppression of the Dáil and the intensification of British pressure the initiative passed very decidedly to the military wing of Sinn Féin. Imprisonments and repressive British action led to a partial weakening in the political wing of Sinn Féin and in the 1920 local elections Sinn Féin did not repeat its general election annihilation of the Parliamentary Party, though it did emerge as the biggest single party. Then in the pre-Truce period with the emphasis more and more on military success and with an increase in British military operations the effectiveness and importance of the political side of Sinn Féin declined somewhat.

The very fact that Sinn Féin was under such pressure prior to the gaining of independence, the fact that few of its leaders had any substantial political experience, and the other factor

4

mentioned earlier—the coalition nature of Sinn Féin, at times an uneasy alliance of military and constitutional groups —all contributed to the uncertainty and ambivalence of the party on the question of the Treaty.

The acceptance of the Treaty by the Dáil and the subsequent rejection of this decision by a sizeable minority within the Sinn Féin parliamentary party signalled the beginning of the end of pre-independence Sinn Féin. By May 1922 the split on the Treaty was causing a state of confusion and paralysis to grip the party, and the party in fact was well on the way to collapse. Local organisations were falling to pieces—feelings on the Treaty were running too high for local branches to meet. The Pact election of 1922 widened the gulf and with the commencement of Civil War hostilities the last blow was struck. The second Sinn Féin party which had done so much to transform Irish politics in the period from the end of 1916 to the start of the Civil War now faded out of the scene.

The lasting achievements of Sinn Féin, apart altogether from its role in the attaining of independence, were considerable. For a start it provided a means of entry to parliamentary politics to a new generation of politicians—a generation which was to maintain its dominance of representation until the late 1950s. Indeed, participation in Sinn Féin, in one way or other, was to become almost a *sine qua non* of entry to the Dáil in the decades after independence.[3] Then too the fact that Sinn Féin was successful ensured that the full potential of action through parliamentary methods was realised and ensured that the constitutional parliamentary tradition of the Home Rule party would be carried on in the new state. This was important, for Sinn Féin had within it both civil and military wings—and had parliamentary methods been completely futile the supremacy of the military wing might have become a real danger. As it was, the principle of civilian control was established—something which was to be of crucial importance in the early years of the new state.

Sinn Féin also played a highly important part in helping

to socialise a whole political generation. It provided a degree of political education and familiarisation with such aspects as campaigning, propaganda and electioneering and helped induct a whole new and hitherto disfranchised generation into the political process. This is particularly important in view of the fact that no election had been held since 1910—and in many areas for many years prior to this—and in view of the fact also that 1918 was the first election in which there was full adult suffrage. Thus a whole generation of first-time voters had their first political experience as Sinn Féin voters and activists, and the experience of this, combined with a realisation of the potential of the ballot-box, may have been instrumental in persuading many to give a further try to constitutional methods once more in the mid-1920s, when the smoke of civil war had cleared away.

*   *   *

The Civil War can be seen as one of the central events in modern Irish history and its effect on the development of the Irish party system was deep and lasting. For a start it shattered the unity of Sinn Féin and the fighting, reprisals and executions of the war destroyed Sinn Féin completely. In July 1922 the party's headquarters in Harcourt Street, Dublin, was closed down completely and the staff paid off. By the beginning of 1923 only 60 of the 1,500 branches were in existence and by June this number had dropped to 16.

During the early stages of the Civil War—that is after the 'Pact' election of 1922—only one political party existed in any formal or organised way, the Labour party. Founded in 1912, it had refrained from contesting the 1918 election, but had had 16 of its 17 candidates elected in the 1922 election. Elsewhere there was confusion with a mixture of Farmers, Independents of various interests, anti-Treatyites of various emphasis and the biggest single group—the supporters of the government. This situation did not persist for very long however—by April 1923 the pro-government T.D.s who were already behaving in the Dáil as a party came together to formally launch the Cumann na nGaedheal party, and

6

though operating under difficult circumstances the anti-Treaty group, now calling itself Sinn Féin, fought the 1923 election as a political party.

The main issue in this election was of course the Treaty and the Civil War and it was around this issue that support polarised giving a dominance to the pro- and anti-Treaty parties. Nevertheless this dominance was far from total and 46 of the 153 seats went to Labour, Farmers and Independents. The most significant point however was that over 66 per cent of the total vote was won by the two Sinn Féin parties, and only once (June 1927) during the subsequent 50 years was this share of the vote to drop below 60 per cent. On occasion it has been as high as 85 per cent and has averaged 75 per cent. Thus, though the balance of distribution of this vote between the two parties was to change radically over the years in favour of the anti-Treatyites, the patterns of support laid down at this election were to prove to be lasting; with the dominance of the two off-shoots of Sinn Féin increasing rather than diminishing with the passage of time.

Another consequence of the Civil War stemmed from the nature of the issues around which it was fought. The fact that the main divisive issue was a largely constitutional and nationalistic one was to mean that such issues were to dominate (and for some politicians exclusively so) political debate in the decades to come and in the process play down to some extent at least economic and social issues—and with this the importance and effectiveness of the Labour party.

The fact too that the Civil War was a family quarrel and as such extremely bitter and unforgiving was to inform the whole tone of political debate and controversy during the ensuing decades. The initial differences and hostilities were exacerbated by the events of the 1920s and were to harden into unshakeable attitudes. As a consequence, political issues assumed a rigidity and a dogmatic quality and positions once taken were not easily altered. The Civil War fixed the issues and determined that henceforth the tone of political debate would be bitter, rigid and unforgiving.

7

Another factor which was to have an extremely important influence on the development of the party system was the decision taken in 1922 to have as the electoral system Proportional Representation. That PR should have been adopted was in no way surprising. It was in line with the extreme democracy of many of the post-Versailles settlements, was regarded as the fairest system of election and it was thought that it would most easily facilitate the representation of minority groups in the Dáil. It was also adopted in Northern Ireland but soon abandoned there in favour of the single-seat straight-vote system which ensured the Unionists an even bigger majority. The presence of PR was to be of particular consequence in the 1920s and 1940s when it facilitated the emergence of smaller parties and considerable numbers of Independents and while it has not prevented the bi-polar development of Irish politics it has made it possible for other groups to secure election and has thus prevented the development of a rigid two-party system.

The presence of organised political parties was to have an extremely important stabilising influence on the early years of the new state. The general election of 1923 removed the Civil War from the battlefield to the ballot-box; the presence of Labour and Farmers' parties in the Dáil between 1923–27 ensured an opposition and helped make a reality of parliament; the fact that although the anti-Treatyites were not prepared to enter the Dáil they were prepared to work within the confines of an organised political party, gave to their actions a discipline and coherence which would not otherwise have been possible; the entry of Fianna Fáil to the Dáil in 1927 meant that henceforth all but a small number of extremists were working within the framework and discipline of an established parliamentary system.

NOTES

[1] Michael Laffin, 'Sinn Féin 1916-21' *Capuchin Annual,* 1970.
[2] *Ibid.*
[3] See John Whyte, *Dáil Deputies.*

2

Cumann na nGaedheal and Fine Gael:

I. *Cumann na nGaedheal*

The signing of the Treaty and the debate which followed it sundered irrevocably the uneasy coalition that had been Sinn Féin, wrecking it completely as a coherent or effective political force and causing a rapid polarisation of support along pro- and anti-Treaty lines. It was on this issue too that the Civil War was fought, and however artificial these divisions may have looked to some later writers they were to prove sufficiently deep and lasting to provide a basis for the two parties which subsequently dominated Irish political life and which persisted long after the divisions which had brought about their existence had become irrelevant.

Cumann na nGaedheal sprang from that part of Sinn Féin which accepted the Treaty and whose leaders formed the government which set about establishing the new Irish Free State. The first leaders of this group were Arthur Griffith and Michael Collins, and then after their deaths in August 1922 William T. Cosgrave.

The anti-Treaty T.D.s boycotted the Dáil but the other groups elected in 1922, the Farmers, Labour and Independents, were agreeable to work within the framework laid down by the Treaty. This agreement on fundamentals, however, did not extend to many specific points in the extensive legislative programme being undertaken by the government and it soon became clear that if the government was going to survive and carry out its plans it would need the backing of a consistent and organised body of supporters.

This support it received from those who had been elected as pro-Treaty T.D.s. Although there was no formal party in existence, one of the first acts of the government was to appoint a Whip to organise its support. Those who took the whip were a recognisable group and were known variously as the 'Government Party', the 'Ministry Party' or the 'Treaty Party', and in parliament at least were behaving as if its members were bound by party rules. Given such a situation it would clearly be only a matter of time before this support was organised on a more formal and permanent basis, and in view of the heavy legislative load and the general uncertainty engendered by the Civil War it would be sooner rather than later.

Thus it was that in early January 1923 shortly after the opening of the Dáil session, a convention of pro-Treaty supporters was held in Dublin to prepare for a new party. The calling of this convention did not arouse much comment, and there was little reason why it should, for the proposals would merely put on a formal and permanent basis what already existed loosely and informally. By this stage the pro-Treatyites —with a recognised and accepted leadership structure, a body of more or less disciplined parliamentary support, an acceptable policy programme and a substantial following among the public at large—had most of the elements of a political party.

In April 1923 the new party was formally launched at a meeting in the Mansion House in Dublin. It took as its name Cumann na nGaedheal—a name which had belonged to a Sinn Féin group in the early years of the century.

The launching of the party was low-key and uncontroversial and in his inaugural speech Cosgrave included among the aims of the party the playing down of class, sectional and denominational differences and the opening of the party to all Irishmen who believed in the Treaty as a basis from which the Free State might develop.[1]

The Civil War ended in May 1923 with the defeat— though by no means the unqualified defeat—of the anti-Treatyites. Three months later a general election was held, and though hostilities had now ceased, the state of the country was very far from settled. Political prisoners were still being arrested and sentenced, sporadic outbreaks of violence were

10

occurring and the whole atmosphere was permeated with a bitterness deeper and more intense than anything which had been known before.

In spite of the background of uncertainty and unrest this election saw a pattern laid down which was to persist for the next half century, with the Treaty parties winning between them 70 per cent of the seats and 67 per cent of the total vote. Cumann na nGaedheal emerged as the biggest single party, with 63 seats, but still substantially short of an over-all majority in the 153 seat Dáil. The anti-Treatyites though pledged to boycotting the Dáil if elected and operating under conditions of great difficulty—many supporters had been interned during or after the Civil War, and 64 of the 85 candidates were unable to address their constituents—managed to win 44 seats.

The failure of any party to win an overall majority is not at all surprising. The system of Proportional Representation with multi-seat constituencies made it easier for small parties or locally strong candidates to secure election. The conditions in the country generally added to the confusion. The major groups had not had time to establish or consolidate effective organisational arrangements and there were still many groups —ex-Unionists, Farmers, supporters of the Irish Party—not prepared to be absorbed into the Sinn Féin parties.

The fact that the 44 Republican T.D.s abstained from the Dáil meant that Cumann na nGaedheal did have an overall majority in the assembly. It was certain to be faced with a wide variety of problems as it set about its task of establishing the institutions and procedures of the new state, restoring law and order, re-opening the channels of trade, asserting civilian control over the army and reducing its size, and the numerous other difficult and mundane tasks associated with the founding of a new state.

Because the only fundamental bond holding the party together in the initial stages was a belief in the acceptance of the Treaty, contradictory and sometimes incompatible views were held within the party and these made it liable to split at times of strain or crisis.

11

Thus it was that the crisis caused by the army mutiny of 1924, and in particular the government's handling of that crisis, led to the resignation from Cumann na nGaedheal of nine T.D.s—including the Minister for Industry and Commerce, Joseph McGrath—and to the foundation of a new party, the National party. The following year a further breakaway occurred when three T.D.s objected to the government's failure over the Boundary Commission and formed a new party, Clann Éireann.[2] Cumann na nGaedheal survived these two crises, defeating the National party candidates in seven out of nine by-elections in 1925 and without ever having to worry unduly about Clann Éireann which disappeared in 1927. The two incidents did however indicate the dangers inherent in Cosgrave's attempt to form a broadly based party.

Nor was the Cabinet itself of one mind on important issues of policy. The resignation of General Mulcahy in 1924 was due, in part at least, to differences between Kevin O'Higgins and himself on the question of civilian control of the army. And later, differences were to develop between the Minister for Posts and Telegraphs, J. J. Walsh, who favoured Protection against the Free Trade views of his colleagues. Walsh expressed his differences openly and on more than one occasion. Without giving notice he resigned completely from politics in 1927 after the dissolution of the Dáil.

The Fourth Dáil was dissolved in the early summer of 1927 and the general election fixed for June. The previous year had seen a number of important political developments including the founding of Fianna Fáil—still pledged to abstention but determined to fight all elections, and organising extensively for that purpose. There had also been the foundation of the National League by Captain Willie Redmond which in addition to appealing to the residual Parliamentary Party support could expect to capitalise on some current discontents.

This election was fought vigorously by all groups and was in fact the first general election to be held under conditions approaching normality. The result proved highly inconclusive with the two major parties falling very short of a possible overall majority and with a proliferation of support for the other parties and groups. Cumann na nGaedheal dropped from 63 to 47 seats—just 3 more than Fianna Fáil, while Labour won 22, Farmers 11, Redmond's party 8 and others 21. Moreover Cumann na nGaedheal's popular vote was only 15,000 higher than that of Fianna Fáil—and 100,000 lower than it had been in 1923. However, the continued abstention of Fianna Fáil from the Dáil ensured that Cosgrave, who had support from Farmers and Independents, was re-elected President of the Executive Council and formed his third administration.

Shortly afterwards on July 10 the Vice-President, Kevin O'Higgins, was assassinated. This ghastly event shocked the Cabinet as nothing had before and it reacted with a stringent Public Safety Act. In addition it prepared an Electoral Amendment Act which in effect would force those who stood for election to give an undertaking to take their seats if elected—the purpose being to force Fianna Fáil out of electoral politics or into the Dáil. The latter course was the one chosen, and shortly afterwards de Valera led his party into the Free State Dáil.

The immediate effect of Fianna Fáil's entry was to remove Cumann na nGaedheal's majority. Negotiations took place between the anti-Cumann na nGaedheal forces and a motion of 'no confidence' in the government was tabled by Labour and the National League. The intention was to defeat the government and replace it with a Labour/National League coalition which would have the support of Fianna Fáil. At the last moment, however, one of the National League members crossed to Cumann na nGaedheal and another—the famous Ald. John Jinks—absented himself, so that the government was saved on the casting vote of the Ceann Comhairle. Clearly however there was little point in trying to continue under such circumstances and shortly afterwards Cosgrave dissolved the Dáil and fixed an election for September.[3]

The entry of Fianna Fáil to the Dáil had changed the whole aspect of Irish politics and in this election the contest was much more a straightforward one between Cosgrave and de Valera. Each party gained considerably at the expense of the smaller parties who were little able to bear the burden of two elections in four months. Also of course the electorate now had a realistic alternative to Cumann na nGaedheal and this, combined with the uncertainty of the previous few months, was to make for further polarisation. Thus Cumann na nGaedheal, though still short of an overall majority, remained the biggest single party with 62 seats. Its popular vote increased by 135,000 to 448,100, just 40,000 more than Fianna Fáil which won 57 seats.

Cosgrave could depend on the support of the Farmers' party and some Independents and so on 11 October 1927 by 76 votes to 70 he was elected President once more and formed his fourth and last administration. The emphasis was now more and more on retrenchment and on consolidating the advances of the previous years. The government, confronted with a strong and unrelenting opposition, was increasingly prone to take actions which were to prove electorally damaging.[4]

Cumann na nGaedheal faced the election of 1932 with confidence, seemingly unaware of the variety of interests its policies of the previous few years had antagonised, and underestimating the progress made by Fianna Fáil since its entry to the Dáil. Thus Cumann na nGaedheal campaigned on its record of achievement pointing to what had been done over the previous decade—the restoration of law and order, the improvements in agriculture, the prudent managing of the nation's finances, the constructive part played by the Free State in Commonwealth affairs, and the successful completion of the Shannon scheme. It sought too to highlight the inexperience of Fianna Fáil, its associations with the Irish Republican Army and to suggest that a Fianna Fáil government would be very much under the influence of the I.R.A. Nor were some of the party's candidates or posters averse from hinting at the danger of a Communist takeover through the I.R.A. should Fianna Fáil come to power.

The 1932 election took place after what was for the most

part a peaceful campaign and the results were to show that while Cumann na nGaedheal with a popular vote of 449,810 had only 3,000 votes less than in 1927, Fianna Fáil's popular vote rose from 411,000 to 566,000, winning for that party 15 new seats. Cumann na nGaedheal dropped from 62 to 57, or 15 fewer than Fianna Fáil. De Valera with the support of Labour and some Independents formed his first Fianna Fáil administration in March 1932 and Cumann na nGaedheal for the first time in the party's history went into opposition.

Fianna Fáil had come to power on the crest of a wave of popular enthusiasm, excitement, intense nationalism and, at times, impatience with those who stood in the way of these enthusiasms. It had a widely proclaimed and radical policy to implement and was determined to do so. It opened the jail gates to release I.R.A. prisoners, refused to pay the land annuities to Britain and as a result saw the start of an Economic War with her. It set about dismantling the Treaty settlement and engaged in fierce controversy and polemics with the British government.

Fianna Fáil had the initiative—it was proposing radical changes and it had enthusiastic and popular support. Cumann na nGaedheal was cast in the role of a dogged opposition, proposing nothing, attacking everything. In addition the popular mood was changing. The I.R.A.'s slogan of 'No Free Speech for Traitors' was becoming increasingly common, a strident note was appearing; many Cumann na nGaedheal supporters were feeling intimidated or went in fear of possible victimisation. Cumann na nGaedheal speakers and the party newspaper, the *United Irishman,* were growing increasingly hysterical about the dangers of the Communist threat. The newly founded Army Comrades Association was taking on itself the role of protector of free speech and vanguard of the anti-Communist movement—and in consequence involving itself in an ever-increasing number of clashes with supporters of Fianna Fáil and the I.R.A.

It was against this background that de Valera called a snap election in January of 1933. De Valera wanted a clear and unequivocal mandate to continue his policies and the

15

struggle with England. He also wanted to forestall the tentative moves which were being made to bring the Centre Party, Cumann na nGaedheal and some Independents together to form a united opposition party. The election took all parties by surprise—and vindicated de Valera's judgement. It was a bitter campaign and saw numerous clashes between supporters of the various parties—usually at Cumann na nGaedheal or Centre Party meetings—and when the results were announced Fianna Fáil had gained a further 5 seats and now a single party, Fianna Fáil, had an overall majority for the first time in the history of the Dáil. Cumann na nGaedheal lost a further 8 seats making for a cumulative loss of 13 seats in under a year.

This second electoral defeat in so short a time was to lead to a certain amount of soul-searching within Cumann na nGaedheal. The *United Irishman* felt for example that the main fault was not one of leadership or policy but a failure to organise properly.[5] Others were beginning to think, though to do no more than that as yet, that perhaps a change of leadership was necessary if de Valera was to be successfully confronted.

Shortly after this election the Army Comrades Association adopted as their uniform the blue shirt and in July with the accession to the leadership of the movement of the former Chief of Police, General Eoin O'Duffy, the movement began to spread rapidly. It changed its name to the National Guard, saw itself as the spearhead of the anti-Communist movement in the country and began to develop along quasi-fascist lines. It was quickly banned by the government which affected to see in it a threat to democratic institutions. The effect of this banning was to bring together the three opposition groups— Cumann na nGaedheal, the Centre Party and the National Guard.[6]

The possibility of a Cumann na nGaedheal-Centre Party merger had been under discussion at this stage but little progress was being made, largely because the Centre Party feared that such a merger would, because of the size and record of Cumann na nGaedheal, effectively mean their absorption into the latter. O'Duffy for his part had loudly proclaimed his independence of all political parties but the fact was that a majority of his followers were traditional Cumann na nGaedheal supporters. Thus the banning of his own movement which put him in an isolated position strengthened the view that a new united anti-Fianna Fáil movement was necessary, and the opportunity to play a leading part in the new party helped bring about his rapid change of mind on the whole question and persuaded him to take part in the negotiations.

For Cumann na nGaedheal the arguments in favour of a merger were mixed. The party had failed in two successive elections, had never succeeded in winning an overall majority of seats and appeared to be losing rather than gaining support. Both in policy and outlook the party held much in common with the members of the Centre Party and many of the Blueshirts' supporters and leaders were already Cumann na nGaedheal voters. It was clear that there was a fragmentation of opposition support and resources which was of benefit to none except Fianna Fáil. On the other hand, Cumann na nGaedheal was expected to enter the new alignment on an equal footing with the other groups and so accept a position disproportionate to its existing strength. Thus even though the Centre Party was little more than a year in existence and had only 11 seats, it was demanding an equal number of officers and a position of equality generally. In addition, both the Centre Party and the Blueshirts made it clear that W. T. Cosgrave was not acceptable as party leader and as a result Cosgrave had to give way as leader to O'Duffy —a man who had no political experience and did not even have a seat in the Dáil.

However the arguments in favour of a new departure were to prove stronger. Some within Cumann na nGaedheal saw the occasion as providing the opportunity to replace Cosgrave with a more dashing and flamboyant type of leader. Others were motivated by a growing sense of fear and insecurity in the face of Fianna Fáil and the I.R.A. and others still saw a merger as a sensible and logical mobilisation of the anti-

17

Fianna Fáil forces. Cosgrave himself was not over-enthusiastic but he was not prepared to stand in the way of the new party. And so a series of meetings was held, followed by conventions of each of the three groups. Preparations were made for the launching of the new party, Fine Gael (United Ireland party), and Cumann na nGaedheal after a lifetime of over ten years was subsumed into this new party.[7]

During its lifetime of ten years the Cumann na nGaedheal party acquired the reputation and appearance of a conservative party. It was determined in its efforts to restore law and order and in its protection of the rights of property. It was prudent in its economic policies and more than cautious in its social policies. These were at all times evolutionary rather than revolutionary, seeking to build on the basis already laid down, as, for example, in its continuation of the earlier Land Acts, or in its adaptation of the existing civil service institutions. And though it had sprung from the separatist Sinn Féin movement it was prepared to advocate co-operation with Britain and to emphasise the benefits to Ireland from active participation in the Commonwealth. In the same way, though it originated from a nationalist movement, its nationalism was less excessive and less exclusive than that of its main rival and it sought to include within its ranks representatives of the Protestant Unionist minority.

It is difficult to be precise about the main sources of its support. As the party which was most likely to ensure stability it won the support of the business and propertied classes, of the bigger farmers and shopkeepers. It was strongest in the Eastern and Midland areas and weakest in counties such as Kerry, Clare and Galway. It had the backing of newspapers such as the *Irish Independent* and the *Cork Examiner* and later of the pro-unionist *Irish Times*. In addition, many of those who supported the party in its initial stages because of a belief in the value of the Treaty, undoubtedly stayed with it during the 1920s and this support cut across class or socio-economic lines.

Cumann na nGaedheal was never a majority party and its failure to attain an overall majority may be attributed to a number of factors. For a start the party system had not settled down in the 1920s, especially since Proportional Representation made it easy for smaller groups to proliferate. In addition the fact that the only common unifying bond holding Cumann na nGaedheal together was acceptance of the Treaty, meant that the party was attempting to hold incompatible groups together. The result was that the party, especially in times of stress, showed a marked tendency to disunity. The fact that a Cumann na nGaedheal government had sanctioned the execution of Irishmen during the Civil War was, in many parts of the country, to provide a strong source of hostility, while the party's identification with the better-off sections of the community may have alienated many, especially in the latter years of the 1920s, when economic conditions were steadily deteriorating. Its Commonwealth participation and co-operation with the Southern unionists was too sudden, too soon and too much for many whose nationalism was of a more full-blooded variety. And finally it was weakened by a series of unpopular enactments and by its own failure to pay as much attention to matters of organisation as its main rival Fianna Fáil.[8]

*　　　　*　　　　*

II Fine Gael

(i) *Phase I. 1933–37*

The Fine Gael party was born of the three-fold merger of Cumann na nGaedheal, the Centre Party and the Blueshirts, and its initial appearance could hardly have come at a more dramatic or exciting period in Irish politics. Under its leader General O'Duffy the new party began vigorously, establishing branches and recruiting members throughout the country, in an atmosphere of energetic excitement which gave every indication that the party was about to establish itself as a major political force.

The founding of Fine Gael brought with it an element of novelty to the Irish political scene. It was the first party to have as a constituent element a youth organisation—the banned and shirted National Guard which had now been reconstituted as the League of Youth. In addition the new party's leader did not have a Dáil seat and some of his closest subordinates were themselves new to parliamentary politics. Finally the new party had included in its very detailed and comprehensive policy document, ideas on the setting up of economic and agricultural corporations—ideas then very popular in a number of European countries.

During this first phase Fine Gael was, or certainly appeared to be, dominated by the spectacular performance of the Blueshirt movement. At first it looked as if the alliance was successful but this soon proved to be an illusion. By the middle of 1934 the involvement of many Blueshirt members in illegal anti-rates agitation (largely as a result of losses sustained due to the loss of a large part of the British market in the Economic War) was embarrassing the more constitutionally-minded members of the Fine Gael executive; O'Duffy was proving to be an extravagant but not very effective leader, his exuberant campaigning was a heavy financial burden and his growing and openly expressed admiration for Hitler and Mussolini caused further unease. Then in July 1934, in spite of loudly optimistic assertions, he failed to lead Fine Gael to victory in the local government elections and shortly afterwards he urged his supporters to adopt extra-legal tactics in their opposition to the government's Economic War policies. These events brought the dissatisfaction with O'Duffy and with his leadership to a head and in September 1934 he resigned as leader of Fine Gael, having held the position for just one year.

O'Duffy's resignation was to plunge Fine Gael into bitter internal conflict, create a great amount of confusion and lead to a minor but bitter split which persisted until 1936.

Meanwhile, at the Fine Gael Ard-Fheis of 1935, W. T. Cosgrave had been unanimously elected to the leadership of the party and in the same year Frank MacDermot, the former Centre Party leader and one of Fine Gael's Vice-Presidents, resigned from the party on a policy issue. With his withdrawal, with the disappearance of O'Duffy and the

20

disintegration of the Blueshirts and with the return of Cosgrave to the party leadership, Fine Gael was beginning to look more like a continuation of Cumann na nGaedheal than like the new party it had set out to become in the heady days of 1933.

Many of the Fine Gael leaders were certain that if it had not been for the appearance of the Blueshirts, freedom of speech and freedom of assembly in the Free State would not have survived. Be that as it may it is clear that the whole episode and especially its finale proved to be a traumatic experience for Fine Gael and took a heavy toll. The party had gambled on O'Duffy as a charismatic alternative to de Valera; the gamble had failed dismally, producing instead of the hoped-for electoral success, confusion, bitterness and financial strain. The quasi-fascist aspect of sections of the movement was to prove an embarrassment in later years, especially in the post-war period, and to provide a steady source of opposition taunts. Most of all, perhaps, the fact that the movement ended in failure was to contribute to the general despondency and helplessness which seemed to overcome Fine Gael in the latter part of the 1930s. With the party's defeat in the 1937 general election (it won 48 seats, 20 fewer than Fianna Fáil) and with the return to office of Fianna Fáil for the third successive time, Fine Gael entered into what were destined to be the eleven most dismal and disastrous years in the history of the party.

(ii) *Phase II. 1937–48*

Fine Gael's position changed little between the elections of 1937 and 1938 except that the party lost a further three seats and was well and truly defeated by Fianna Fáil, which received a safe overall majority and in the process became the first party in the Free State ever to get more than 50 per cent of the total votes cast.

The outbreak of war in 1939 further strengthened Fianna Fáil's position. The sense of collective danger and national emergency heightened the need for strong government and worked to the advantage of the party in power. The mood of the country was emphatically against Irish intervention and this was reflected in the support of all parties for de Valera's declaration of Irish neutrality. Fine Gael's attitude on this question could not, because of its strong advocacy of Commonwealth participation, be as unequivocal as the other parties and disagreement with the policy in 1942 was to lead to the resignation from the party of one of its Vice-Presidents, James Dillon.

The only serious or deep-seated opposition to the government's war-time policies came from the I.R.A. The fact that the opposition parties were in agreement with the government on the over-riding issue of the day, combined with the sense of shared danger and the general participation in the defence effort, made it difficult for the opposition parties to function strongly during the war years. Their freedom was still further circumscribed by the imposition of war-time censorship, by the shortage of newsprint which reduced the newspapers to a four-page format and by the petrol rationing which curtailed the holding of political meetings.

But even in spite of these restrictions there was evidence of growing dissatisfaction with the performance of Fianna Fáil and in the general election of 1943 this dissatisfaction found expression in the support given to the new Clann na Talmhan party and in the record vote picked up by the Labour party, especially in Dublin. Fianna Fáil lost 10 seats in this election, but instead of being able to capitalise on this Fine Gael lost 13 seats and was now reduced to 32 seats. Fianna Fáil was still by far the dominant party and de Valera formed his fifth successive administration.

In 1944 Cosgrave retired as leader of Fine Gael. He had been less successful as leader of the party in opposition than he had been as head of government. Fine Gael had survived but had not prospered. In fairness it must be said that he had assumed the leadership at a time when the party was split, divided and weakened by the Blueshirt episode, and that later the outbreak of war had the effect of dampening political controversy and making more difficult the task of effective opposition.

Cosgrave was succeeded as party leader by General Richard Mulcahy—the man who had succeeded Collins as Chief-of-Staff in 1922 and who had been first choice among some members of the Cabinet at that time for head of government also. Mulcahy had been a minister in the early and again in the later 1920s, and later in the 1930s he had been active in the Blueshirts. As far as his political opponents were concerned, his having been Chief-of-Staff during the Civil War made him a highly controversial figure and the object of considerable bitterness. Thus the fact that the leadership of Fine Gael was now passing to a man so closely associated with the controversies and bitterness of the 1920s was of some significance for it meant that as far as Fine Gael was concerned there would be no real attempt to break out of the old moulds and that the party would continue to be dominated by the issues and leaders of the past.

As a result the advent of Mulcahy to the leadership made little appreciable change either in the personnel, the policies or the fortunes of the party. If anything the situation deteriorated yet further. In the election of May 1944 the party put forward only 57 candidates (an open admission that it had ceased to see itself as capable of forming a government) and won only 30 seats. Its popular vote of 250,000 was considerably less than half of that secured by Fianna Fáil and the only consolation from otherwise dismal results was the return to the Dáil of Mulcahy and John A. Costello, both of whom had lost their seats in 1943.[9]

The immediate post-war period was characterised by shortages, continuing austerities, rising prices and strikes and there was evidence of growing discontent (and boredom) with a government which had been in power continuously since 1932. Fine Gael however had little success in capitalising on this discontent; in fact at times it hardly seemed to have even the inclination to do so. The party had reached the stage where it had ceased to contest most by-elections. The political initiative was now firmly with the new Clann na Poblachta party which was apparently about to emerge as a major political force. It was to prevent Clann na Poblachta from consolidating its by-election gains that de Valera called a general election for February 1948.

Fine Gael faced this election without any great expectations though it did increase its number of candidates to 82. Its popular vote remained almost as before, but for the first time in over a decade the downward trend was arrested—but only just. The party's Dáil strength rose from 30 to 31.

This election however saw the disappearance of Fianna Fáil's overall majority and saw too a proliferation of minor parties and Independents. This time Fianna Fáil could not expect to win the support of these groups and Mulcahy, as the leader of the biggest non-Fianna Fáil party, took the initiative in seeking to form an inter-party government. (Earlier in the 1940s Fine Gael had urged the formation of such a government.) There were some obstacles in the way of such a creation—Clann na Poblachta's Republicanism and Fine Gael's Free Statism were thought by some to be incompatible; Labour and Fine Gael were by tradition mutually antipathetic; Labour was split. These difficulties however were overcome and the final impediment—the unacceptability of Mulcahy as head of government—was removed when he proposed as leader John A. Costello. He was acceptable to all parties and so with him as Taoiseach the first inter-party government became a reality in the early months of 1948.

The years 1937–48 had been disastrous for Fine Gael but now, almost unexpectedly, the party was given an opportunity to arrest what looked like an inevitable and fatal decline.

(iii) *Phase III. 1948–57*

Of all the parties which took part in the inter-party experiment Fine Gael was the one which benefited most. In electoral terms the downward plunge of the '30s and '40s was arrested and the party was to experience a limited but very real revival, rising to 40 seats in 1951 and 50 in 1954. In the process it was to win the allegiance of some prominent Independent T.D.s including its former Vice-President James Dillon who rejoined the party in 1952. It also recruited some new talent and set about organising its finances and party structure.[10] In addition participation in government enhanced the image and morale of the party. The fact that the Taoiseach was of the Fine Gael party was good both for the prestige of party and leader. This injection of new life and hope could not have come at a more crucial time for it is extremely doubtful if the party could have survived another long, unrelieved spell in opposition.

Apart from demonstrating that there was a workable alternative government to Fianna Fáil (which in the long term may well have been its most important achievement) the first inter-party government was significant for three main episodes—the declaration of a 26 County Republic in 1949, the Mother and Child controversy and the adoption of Keynesian theories of capital expenditure.[11] Costello proved sympathetic to the application of Keynesian doctrines on government spending to Irish conditions; the declaration of the Republic may have been inconsistent with Fine Gael's more recent stance but there is no evidence to suggest that it alienated any significant section of the party's support. Even the acrimonious Mother and Child controversy, which precipitated the collapse of the government, did little permanent damage to Fine Gael—the main sufferer clearly was the Clann na Poblachta party.

The three years in government had revived Fine Gael in a way few could have thought possible and in the election of 1951 the party reached the respectable total of 40 seats and 342,000 first preference votes. The years 1951–54 were unspectacular, indeed dull, years and Fine Gael found itself back in its familiar opposition role. Now however with the experience of government behind it, with its Dáil forces augmented, it was more confident in its own ability and displayed much greater spirit than had been the case in the 1940s.

In the 1954 election Fine Gael campaigned on an inter-party ticket and won 50 seats (427,000 votes). It was now stronger than at any time since its foundation twenty years earlier. In this election Fianna Fáil dropped to 65 seats, so Fine Gael and Labour (18) and Clann na Talmhan (5) formed the second inter-party government (and had the support but not the participation of Clann na Poblachta). This time Fine Gael was in a much more dominant position and in addition to a Fine Gael Taoiseach supplied eight members of the Cabinet.

In spite of the greater experience of the Cabinet and the stronger position of Fine Gael within the government the second inter-party period was less happy than the first had been, largely because of the range of external problems which faced the government. No more than Fianna Fáil during its term of office after the War or between 1951–4 was the new government able to damp down inflation. The remedies (cutting public expenditure and increasing taxation) showed little imagination, were not particularly effective, but won for the government widespread unpopularity. In addition the government was faced with a revival of I.R.A. activity which included arms raids on military barracks in Northern Ireland and England, followed by a series of attacks on police barracks and customs posts in the six-counties. The government reacted by attempting to impose the full rigours of the law on apprehended I.R.A. men, but this attempted firmness was to cause Seán MacBride to withdraw his support from the government early in 1957 and precipitate a general election.

Thus while Fine Gael may have been left unscathed by the controversies of the first inter-party period that was not to be the case on this occasion. The worsening economic situation produced conditions of near panic with rising unemployment and a sharp increase in emigration. This situation was capitalised on by Fianna Fáil which according to one later description was proving to be a 'roust-about, riproaring opposition'[12] and the memory of these years was to prove damaging to Fine Gael during the boom-time elections of the late 1960s. The strong anti-I.R.A. line could hardly be said to have lost Fine Gael much of its traditional support but it did have the effect of reactivating some of the residual anti-Cumann na nGaedheal Republicanism which could at times be quite virulent.

It was in conditions of some bitterness and not a little desolation that Fine Gael faced the 1957 election. Not surprisingly the gains of 1954 were wiped out and the party dropped back to 40 seats losing 100,000 votes in the process. Fianna Fáil with 78 seats now had a comfortable overall majority and Mr de Valera set about forming his eighth—and last—administration. For Fine Gael this was indeed a severe set-back, but at least the idea of inter-party co-operation was still intact, and with it the possibility of offering a strong and credible alternative to Fianna Fáil.

(iv) *Phase IV. Post 1957*

Relations between Fine Gael and its main inter-party partner, Labour, remained cordial during the early years of the new Fianna Fáil government. This cordiality was in no way threatened by the election of a new Fine Gael leader in 1959, for the new leader, Mr James Dillon, had been a successful and enthusiastic member of the two inter-party governments and a strong supporter of the whole concept of inter-party government. This support was shared by the Labour leader William Norton but in 1961 when he retired and was succeeded by Mr Brendan Corish a perceptible change occurred. Although Mr Corish had been a member of the two inter-party governments he was becoming dubious about the prospect of another such partnership and under his leadership Labour opted for an independent strategy in the elections of 1965 and 1969. The adoption of this strategy was hardly a success as far as Labour was concerned but it contributed greatly to the frustration of Fine Gael during these years by confirming the Fianna Fáil claim that it was the only party capable of winning enough support to form a government.

Fine Gael was destined to remain in opposition for the entire duration of the 1960s. Although the party was to make some impressive gains, the prolonged absence from office, the failure to reach a modus vivendi with Labour, defeat in three successive elections and the party's inability to dislodge a traumatically divided and weakened Fianna Fáil party after the arms crisis of 1970–71, were to produce a sense of helplessness and frustration among many of the party's leading members and supporters. Thus while the party's Dáil strength rose from 40 in 1957 to 47 in 1961, remained at 47 in 1965 and moved to 50 in 1969 and while the popular vote in the same period was to rise from 326,700 (1957) to 375,000 (1961), to 427,000 (1965) to 450,000 (1969) these gains were not sufficiently large to disturb the balance between the three main parties, and were made in fact, not at the expense of Fianna Fáil or Labour but at the expense of the smaller parties and Independents who virtually disappeared from the scene during these years. Fine Gael's big successes during this period were the major part it played in successfully leading the campaign against the government's attempt to abolish PR in 1959 and 1968, and in the spectacular presidential campaign of Mr T. F. O'Higgins in 1966 who lost the Presidency to Mr de Valera by only 10,000 votes out of a total poll of over one million. These successes—or near successes—heartening though they were, brought Fine Gael no nearer the reality of power and the party was forced to remain in stranded opposition.

Nor was Fine Gael helped by the rising affluence and unprecedented economic boom of the 60s. Fianna Fáil as the party in power benefited most from this and indeed was able to represent Fine Gael, which could not hope to form a government on its own and had no prospect, either, of forming an inter-party government, as a potential threat to this new-found prosperity. In addition the fact that in the 1960s the emphasis in Irish politics shifted from the old nationalistic and constitutional issues to concentrate more and more on social and economic ones meant that Fine Gael was unable to find any great or divisive issue on which it might mobilise support and base a distinctive campaign against Fianna Fáil. Northern Ireland had all but ceased to be a political issue in Southern politics up to 1969. All parties were agreed on the need for unification through peaceful means but went little further than stating this hope. On the question of Ireland's membership of the European Economic

Community, Fine Gael supported the government's decision to apply for membership. On other matters Fine Gael's differences with the government were largely on questions of detail and emphasis and there were no indications of any fundamental cleavages. The two parties had after all a common parentage in the old Sinn Féin party and in spite of having developed along very different lines in the early stages now appeared to be moving closer and closer (if not in terms of cordiality at least in terms of attitudes and policies). Both parties appeared to be travelling along the same road—the main difference being that Fianna Fáil seemed to be travelling faster and enjoying the journey better.

In many ways Fine Gael passed through the 1960s unsure of the role it should be playing in Irish politics and this uncertainty was reflected in the frequent internal differences in the party. The strain between the hitherto dominant conservative wing and a younger group (led by Mr Declan Costello), seeking to persuade the party to adopt more progressive social and economic policies, was to be a recurring feature of the party especially during the middle years of the 1960s. The younger group scored what looked like a major victory when the party adopted a new policy *The Just Society* shortly before the 1965 election. This however had little electoral consequence. The 'conversion' of the Old Guard was too sudden to be convincing and it was clear that many leading members were not wholehearted in their support. The controversy was far from finished and while the party was never faced with an actual split the underlying tension was to exhibit itself on a number of other subsequent occasions.

Mr James Dillon resigned as party leader immediately after the 1965 election. His resignation was in no sense forced on him—he wanted to give his successor ample time to prepare for the next election and for that reason he decided to withdraw to the back benches. He was succeeded by Mr Liam T. Cosgrave, son of the late W. T. Cosgrave. Under his leadership Fine Gael made quiet but undramatic progress. The Fine Gael candidate came close to winning the

1966 presidential election and the Fine Gael-Labour alliance defeated the government's attempt to change the voting system in 1968. Attempts were made to improve the organisational structure of the party, develop its policies and recruit new members, and in the Dáil the party adopted a more vigorous approach than before. The first electoral test of the new leader showed however that while the party pushed its first preference vote up to 450,000, won 50 seats and gained some energetic and able new members in both Dáil and Senate, it still failed to make any significant inroads on the Fianna Fáil position and in addition showed a tendency to lose still further ground in some of the expanding Dublin constituencies.

The Northern crisis which threw Fianna Fáil into disarray and threatened the survival of the government left Fine Gael virtually unscathed. The party failed to capitalise on the opportunities presented to defeat Fianna Fáil and at the same time had its own future made less certain by the re-entry into Southern politics of the most unpredictable of all factors—the Northern issue.

Sources of Support

Fine Gael began its life with a great deal of 'inherited' support—not surprisingly since it was an amalgam of three existing groups. From Cumann na nGaedheal it got the support of the business and commercial classes, the bigger farmers, shopkeepers, much of the Protestant community and of course those who had given their allegiance to Cumann na nGaedheal because of their belief in the Treaty. The presence of the Centre Party ensured the support of the farming community. From the beginning it is accurate to say that in general Fine Gael's main support came essentially from the middle classes, though not exclusively so by any means. But it was, in the context of the 1930s, much more representative of the middle classes than either Fianna Fáil or Labour.

Fine Gael's electoral record between the time of its foundation and 1948 is one of steady decline, dropping from

30

460,000 votes in 1937 to 250,000 in 1944. It is not possible to say with any certainty from what areas its support was declining, but there are a number of possible answers. Apart from natural wastages—death and emigration especially—the party was undoubtedly losing ground to Fianna Fáil among the business classes, who by now were satisfied of Fianna Fáil's 'non-revolutionary' nature and some of whom were benefiting from Fianna Fáil's protectionist policies. Fine Gael also undoubtedly lost ground among some of its farming supporters to the new Clann na Talmhan party while the dangers of war after 1939 may have persuaded others to opt for the one party capable of providing strong, stable government during those perilous years. Then the Blueshirt episode may have disillusioned some supporters while the lack-lustre, spiritless performance of the party in the 1940s was not likely to give it much appeal to younger voters. Indeed Fine Gael was in every sense an ageing party in the 1940s and it probably had little capacity to recruit new, younger voters. The part played by Fine Gael in the declaration of the Republic in 1949 may have lost the party some of its traditional ex-Unionist and Protestant supporters.

In more recent times it has not been possible to say exactly from which sectors Fine Gael derives most of its support, because no major studies have been undertaken on the sources of support of the various parties. However, one important recent survey (Gallup Poll, Dublin, April 1969—details, Appendix A) does reinforce the view of Fine Gael as a predominantly middle-class and middle-aged party. The survey found for example that whereas Fianna Fáil's support came almost in equal proportions from middle-class and working-class voters, and Labour's was predominantly working-class, Fine Gael had a much higher proportion of middle-class voters than working-class. The survey found also that Fine Gael drew heavily on the farming community. Among the bigger farmers and especially among those who were members of a farming organisation, Fine Gael was stronger than Fianna Fáil but among the smaller farmers the opposite was the case. The image of Fine Gael as an ageing party was

31

also strengthened by the findings of this poll. It found that while Fianna Fáil's support was evenly distributed, Labour was disproportionately stronger among younger voters, especially younger working-class voters, and Fine Gael was disproportionately represented among the older voters.

Findings such as these must of their very nature be tentative and a great deal of further research would be necessary to locate with accuracy the exact nature of the support accorded Fine Gael, but even in their tentative state the figures would seem to confirm to some extent at least the image of Fine Gael as a conservative and middle-class party—adjectives often applied to it by its opponents.

*　　　*　　　*

Fine Gael could not be described as a particularly successful political party. Although it has been in existence for nearly 40 years it has never held office on its own, and on only two three-year occasions during that time has it shared office— albeit as the major partner. Most of its lifetime has been spent on the Opposition benches and this inevitably has had an effect on the morale and approach of its members.

It is possible to locate some of the factors which have contributed to this situation. It inherited the anti-Republican and pro-Commonwealth image of Cumann na nGaedheal, an image which was particularly damaging in some of the western counties. Its middle-class image, again partly in-herited from Cumann na nGaedheal and in part a result of its support from the bigger farmers, harmed it among working-class voters. The participation of the Centre Party continued the image of the party as being a big farmers' party and damaged it among the small western farmers. (Thus it was Clann na Talmhan and not Fine Gael which profited by their discontent in the early 1940s.) The Blue-shirt episode was harmful both to the morale and image of the party and the difficulties of waging strong opposition during the War years further weakened the party. In opposition in the '40s some of its members tended to become almost obsessed with Civil War issues and this in part ex-plains the stale and jaded nature of the party's policy offering

32

during these years. Moreover Fine Gael has never been organised as extensively or as thoroughly nor displayed the same degree of professionalism as Fianna Fáil so consistently has. The approach of the party, especially in the late 1950s and early 1960s, was frequently castigated by critics (some within the party) for its amateur, easy-going, almost half-hearted and part-time approach to the question of attaining power.

All of these factors have contributed to Fine Gael's apparently chronic inability to lift itself out of its secondary position, for while it has displayed over the years a remarkable capacity for survival, it has demonstrated an equally remarkable inability to successfully tackle Fianna Fáil. Perhaps the basic cause of this incapacity lies in the nature of Fianna Fáil's support—the fact that Fianna Fáil draws its support in almost even amounts from virtually every section of the population. Thus while Fine Gael may be characterised as essentially a middle-class and farmers' party, it has to fight hard to equal Fianna Fáil's support from these very areas, while at the same time it has nowhere like Fianna Fáil's ability to attract working-class support.

NOTES

[1] K. Hancock, *Survey of British Commonwealth Affairs,* Vol. 1, 323-4.
[2] See ch. 5 below.
[3] For a full and amusing account of this episode see *Sunday Press* Dec. 1971, article by Proinsias MacAonghusa.
[4] See essay by K. B. Nowlan 'President Cosgrave's Last Administration' in MacManus ed. *The Years of the Great Test.*
[5] See M. Manning, *The Blueshirts,* 212.
[6] For a full discussion of this period and further references see Manning, *op. cit.*
[7] *Ibid.*
[8] Nowlan, *op. cit.*
[9] Essay in Nowlan and Williams, *Ireland in the War Years and After.*
[10] It was only now that Fine Gael began to have a national collection.
[11] For a full discussion of this inter-party period see Lyons, *op. cit.,* 552-80, and also J. H. Whyte, *Church and State in Modern Ireland 1923-70.*
[12] *Irish Times* editorial, January 1972.

3

Fianna Fáil

The dominance of Fianna Fáil on the political life of the Irish state over the last forty years has been almost complete. In the period since 1932 Fianna Fáil has been in office for all but six years and in that time has formed eleven of the thirteen governments; its candidates have won every contested presidential election; its percentage share of the popular vote during this time has never dropped below 40 per cent and at times has been as high as 52 per cent. Its record of success has accustomed it to regarding itself as a 'natural' majority or government party and it is perhaps one of the ironies of modern Irish history that the party which began its life as an abstentionist 'slightly constitutional'[1] party, based on the defeated Civil War group, should end up in this position.

(i) *Prelude: The Third Sinn Féin Party 1923–26*[2]

In May 1923 the Civil War came to an end with the defeat of the anti-Treaty forces. This defeat was far from total and within a matter of weeks attempts were being made to organise a political movement dedicated to the establishment of a Republic around the available anti-Treaty groups. In particular the question arose as to whether or not the anti-Treatyites should contest the general election which was expected shortly. By this time the pro-Treaty group had organised itself into the Cumann na nGaedheal party. The Labour and Farmers' parties were also in existence and so at a series of informal meetings in May it was decided to re-organise Sinn Féin as a political party (a decision which drew some protests from former members of Sinn Féin who had taken the Treaty side).

34

The circumstances surrounding the formation of this new party could hardly have been less favourable—the Civil War lost, thousands of supporters in jail and morale at a low ebb. It was in such circumstances that the new party had to set about tackling the immediate task of contesting an election and the more long-term job of building up a nation-wide organisation.

The election took place in August and in spite of harassment and the fact that over 12,000 Republicans were in jail (including de Valera who was arrested during the campaign) Sinn Féin managed to put forward 85 candidates. Notwithstanding the adverse circumstances and its abstentionist policy the party won 300,000 first preference votes and 44 seats. It was clear from this result that the new party would have a strong basis from which to build as soon as some sort of normality was restored.

The policy of abstention was rigidly adhered to by this group and over the next few years attempts were made to establish a Republican Dáil and to duplicate the functions of the 'usurping' Free State assembly, especially by providing judicial and educational services.

Within a year of the ending of the Civil War the great majority of prisoners were released and this was to give a tremendous boost to the development of the new party. Sympathetic Irish groups in the United States made funds available, a central office was set up, paid organisers hired and the support of the I.R.A. was offered. Attempts were made, successfully, to reactivate many of the old Sinn Féin clubs throughout the country and in addition many of those who had been jailed after the Civil War had used their time in jail to prepare themselves for just this kind of political activity.

The rate of progress during the first year of the party's existence was remarkable. Apart from the election of 44 T.D.s, who provided a ready-made nucleus of leaders, the establishment of new branches proceeded rapidly. By the time of the first Ard-Fheis in October 1923, 680 branches were established. The following month this figure had risen to 729 and the process was to continue throughout 1924. There were also the attempts already mentioned to duplicate the function of the Free State government, though these were not particularly successful. Attempts were made too to establish a regular newspaper, to organise publicity and to educate members in the art of political campaigning and electoral work. In fact according to Mr Peter Pyne[3] the party sought to be much more than a mere political party: 'It did not confine its attentions exclusively to politics of a parliamentary nature, but attempted to isolate its adherents as far as possible from the influence of what it regarded as a usurping State.'

The early progress and initial success of the party were not to be maintained. This was partly due to its inability to successfully duplicate or substitute for the functions of the Free State government. More particularly it was due to the policy of abstention which isolated the party from the real centres of power, prevented its leaders from playing any effective role in the development of the new state, strengthened the position of Cumann na nGaedheal in the Dáil, reduced the Sinn Féin T.D.s to the role of shadow-boxers and cut off the followers of Sinn Féin from any possibility of patronage or preference in the allocation of jobs.

The reality of this situation was soon to become apparent to some of the more pragmatic members of the party and especially to such as Seán Lemass and Gerry Boland. During 1924 the party began to decline in strength and this decline continued through 1925 and into 1926. Financial support for the party dried up; the staffing of the central office had to be cut; the support of the I.R.A. was withdrawn; the number of branches decreased—and all the while the Free State was functioning, enacting legislation and being recognised by foreign powers. Within Sinn Féin the sense of futility increased and was heightened by the party's inability at the end of 1925 to influence the Boundary Award which effectively made the partition of Ireland permanent. More and more Sinn Féin was becoming a helpless spectator.

It is clear that by 1925 Mr de Valera was becoming conscious of the need for a change in strategy and was moving

36

to a position where the Oath of Allegiance[4] was to become the main obstacle. Thus in January 1926 he announced that if the oath were to go he would be prepared to enter the Dáil and later at the Sinn Féin Ard-Fheis a motion in de Valera's name declared 'that once the admission oaths of the 26 and 6 county assemblies are removed, it becomes a question not of principle but of policy whether or not Republican representatives should attend these assemblies'. This motion was to precipitate a major split in Sinn Féin when the Ard-Fheis met in March 1926. After two days of debate de Valera's motion was defeated by 223 votes to 218. Shortly afterwards he resigned as President of Sinn Féin and what proved to be the last Ard-Fheis of that party came to an end.

The life of the party was now rapidly drawing to a close. From this point on there was a steady drift from Sinn Féin to the de Valera side and soon the party was split down the middle—its Standing Committee, its Dáil deputies, its office staff and its cumainn—and this trend to de Valera accelerated a few months later in May 1926 when he formally launched his new Fianna Fáil party.

The resignation of de Valera and the defection of his supporters was to mark the end of Sinn Féin as a major political force. It is possible that some of de Valera's supporters welcomed the opportunity of founding a new and more flexible party and the opportunity too to shake off some of the more 'impractical', idealistic and dogmatic personalities who dominated to such an extent in the old party. As Pyne notes, 'After March 1926 the party known as Sinn Féin bore little resemblance to the party that had gone before it, having only a minor organisation on the fringe of the political scene, with little prospect of ever gaining power by constitutional means. The Fourth Sinn Féin party was the last remains of a major party that had passed away, like a fossil telling of pre-historic times. Denied a reasonable chance of ever forming a government, with the responsibility this would entail, it became more extreme and more intransigent in its attitudes.'[5]

In the last chapter it was noted that Cumann na nGaedheal at this stage drew most of its support from the established classes, the bigger farmers, the business community, the Unionist or ex-Unionist minority and that it was, as a rule, stronger in the east than in the west. It is possible to be even more precise about the nature of Sinn Féin support during these years thanks to the exhaustive study already mentioned.[6]

Sinn Féin it would seem obtained much of its support from the west and south-west, from rural areas with small urban populations, and from constituencies with a tradition of radicalism. It had the support too of the less well-off sections of the agricultural community, and especially in areas where emigration was highest.

The party was little supported by city dwellers, university graduates, Protestants and large farmers. Nor was it strongly supported by the industrial workers or by non-agricultural workers throughout the country. And according to the U.S. political scientist Warner Moss, the support of the landless labourers went to the Labour party. Thus in short Sinn Féin from 1923 to 1926 'was largely the party of the rural lower middle class, the owner-occupiers and small shop-keepers and traders, the party of the people who were, perhaps, the most vulnerable to economic recession'.[7]

(ii) *Fianna Fáil 1926–32*

The Fianna Fáil party which was founded in the La Scala Theatre, Dublin, in May 1926 began its life with a number of advantages rarely given to a new party. In one sense Fianna Fáil was less a new party than the regrouping of forces which had been tried and moulded over the previous decade and the direction of the new party was in the hands of men who were fast acquiring an expertise and professionalism in their approach to questions of political organisation.

The new party began with a ready-made leadership structure. Its first President and undisputed leader was Eamon de Valera, a man who had been in the very forefront of Irish politics since 1916, enjoyed even at this stage enormous personal prestige and support throughout the country and was an astute political strategist. He was to prove a charismatic leader and one of the biggest single influences on the development and continued growth of Fianna Fáil. For many, between now and his retirement over thirty years later, he personified Fianna Fáil.

But the new party was in no sense a one-man party. De Valera dominated but did not overshadow his leading supporters, many of whom had earned reputations for themselves during the Anglo-Irish and Civil Wars. For the most part they were men of strong individuality and were to blend together as a cohesive team in the decades to come. Even at this stage names such as Seán T. O'Kelly, Frank Aiken, Dr James Ryan, Seán Lemass, Seán MacEntee and P. J. Ruttledge were known throughout the country and each had gained considerable practical experience in the techniques of political organisation in the Second and Third Sinn Féin parties.

The new party, although abstentionist, had a body of elected public representatives inherited from the election of 1923. From the start the party could speak with authority, and the presence of the T.D.s made all the easier the establishment of constituency organisations. In many cases too the Sinn Féin cumainn were reactivated as Fianna Fáil clubs; many of the members of these clubs were already experienced party workers, thus removing the necessity of beginning local re-organisation completely from scratch.

In addition the new party came into being secure in the knowledge that it could expect to inherit a sizeable and dependable body of support. The election of 1923 had demonstrated the persistence of a strong Republican sentiment even in the face of Civil War defeat. Fianna Fáil, as the only major Republican party, could expect to secure the bulk of this support, thus giving it a strong basis from which to operate.

Fianna Fáil had one further advantage. From the very start it had a clear and distinctive personality and was in no sense a carbon copy of any existing party. It was an avowedly and unequivocally Republican party and as such was filling a vacuum which could not be filled by the Free State party,

Cumann na nGaedheal, by the Farmers or by the Labour party. So it did not face the problem which frequently confronts new parties—that of finding a distinctive identity and issues around which to polarise support. It had them already.

Fianna Fáil was quick to consolidate these early advantages. It set about developing its social and economic policies but in particular, under the direction of Seán Lemass and Gerald Boland, it set about building up a nationwide network of branches, moulding them into an active, disciplined and highly efficient organisation and in the process laying the foundations of a structure that was to sustain Fianna Fáil in power in the years ahead.

In spite of the manifest progress of this first year, Fianna Fáil still had one very serious defect—the fact that it was still an abstentionist party, working outside of the parliamentary process and unlikely therefore to be in a position to assume power or influence policy. The futility of such a position was undoubtedly an important deterrent for many moderate voters who might otherwise have been prepared to support the new party.

The fact also that the party was outside of Parliament, combined with the Civil War record of many of its leaders and the ties of friendship which existed between the party and the I.R.A., ensured that it was still less than acceptable to many of the propertied and business classes. Indeed there were many during these years who saw Fianna Fáil as a dangerous if not revolutionary threat to the stability of the state.[8]

Fianna Fáil's first electoral test was in the general election of June 1927. Before the election de Valera visited the United States of America on a fund raising trip and the party set about nominating 87 candidates. The party rejected I.R.A. overtures about the formation of a new Republican front and its election literature, apart from attacking the Oath of Allegiance and pledging the establishment of a Republic, urged the imposition of protective tariffs, the negotiation of a new financial settlement with Great Britain and a cessation of the land-annuity payments to Britain.

The election campaign saw the bitterness of the Civil War

40

period come to the surface once more but the election itself had an entirely inconclusive result. Fianna Fáil improved hardly at all on the position of Sinn Féin in 1923 and won 44 seats—just three fewer than Cumann na nGaedheal.

Fianna Fáil however still refused to enter the Dáil and Cosgrave was re-elected though without a secure majority. Then on 10 July came the assassination of Kevin O'Higgins and the reaction of the government in the shape of a new Public Safety Act and the Electoral Amendment Bill. This latter was aimed specifically at Fianna Fáil's policy of contesting elections but refusing to enter the Dáil. The Bill provided that every candidate for election to either House should, when nominated, swear that if elected he would take the oath as prescribed by the Constitution. Every elected member who failed to do this within a given time would be disqualified and his seat vacated.

Already by this stage two members of the Fianna Fáil parliamentary party had taken the oath but Mr de Valera himself had firmly declared just a few weeks earlier that he would never 'take the oath of allegiance to a foreign king'. However, faced with the alternative of electoral incapacity the party altered its earlier stand, the oath became no more than an empty political formula and Fianna Fáil entered the Dáil.

In spite of the humiliation of the occasion it is very probable that the majority of members were relieved that this had come about. Certainly Fianna Fáil's decision altered the balance dramatically and meant that now for the first time the defeated Civil War group was in a position to attain political power.

Shortly after Fianna Fáil's entry to the Dáil Cosgrave ordered a dissolution and fixed a general election for September. In this election the contest became much more a straight fight between Fianna Fáil and Cumann na nGaedheal, each of which was capable of forming a government. The smaller parties, all in financial straits, and the National League, discredited as well, were relegated to a secondary role. No party won an overall majority, but each of the major parties improved its position considerably. Fianna Fáil gained thirteen seats to give it a total of 57 and establish it securely as the second biggest party with just five seats fewer than Cumann na nGaedheal.

Fianna Fáil's acceptance of constitutionality and entry into the Dáil was to strengthen it enormously and the years 1927–32 were to be years of steady and sustained growth for the party. As the election results of September 1927 would seem to demonstrate there was a substantial number of voters anxious to support Fianna Fáil but not prepared to waste their votes on an abstentionist candidate. More than that the polarisation of issues which followed Fianna Fáil's entry into the Dáil was to benefit the two major parties.

Once in the Dáil Fianna Fáil lost no time in establishing itself as a tough and unyielding opposition and Dáil exchanges which had been comparatively low-keyed, almost impersonal, before 1927 now assumed a new intensity, and a degree of personal bitterness, hitherto absent, began to appear. On one occasion, in March 1930, Fianna Fáil managed to defeat the government in a Dáil vote on the Old Age Pensions Bill. In a subsequent vote of confidence however the position of the Cosgrave government was reaffirmed.

Outside the Dáil the party continued to build up its organisation with this work, as before, being directed by Seán Lemass and Gerald Boland. In 1931 with the establishment of the *Irish Press* the party had its own newspaper and at a time when radio was still in its infancy and newspapers were the most influential medium of communication the importance of this development can hardly be over-estimated. Up to now the other daily papers, the unionist *Irish Times*, the Catholic middle-class *Irish Independent* and the *Cork Examiner* had been solid in their hostility to Fianna Fáil but with the establishment of the *Irish Press* the party now had its own partisan newspaper—and one which before long had a circulation of close on 100,000.

Fianna Fáil benefited also during those years from the unpopular decisions of the Cumann na nGaedheal government and especially from the proposals of that government in the early 1930s, to deal with the economic crisis—proposals

42

which envisaged cuts of ten per cent in all public service salaries and a cut of one shilling in the old age pension. These proposals certainly alienated large sections of the public and such alienation was bound to work to the advantage of Fianna Fáil.

The extent of the progress made by Fianna Fáil during these years was not always obvious to its opponents. It is certain that the Cosgrave government, pre-occupied with its own problems, underestimated it and were unprepared for the large gains Fianna Fáil were soon to make in the election of 1932. In any event it can be said with certainty that Fianna Fáil used the years in opposition between 1927 and 1932 to extremely good effect, and it was a much stronger, more confident Fianna Fáil which faced the general election called for March 1932.

(iii) *Fianna Fáil 1932–48*

Fianna Fáil approached the election of 1932 secure in the knowledge that the Republican vote safely belonged to it. As a result the party's policy statement was able to treat the issue of the Republic in a low-keyed fashion and concentrate on reassuring the moderate voters, the uncommitted and those disillusioned with Cumann na nGaedheal, that Fianna Fáil was in every sense a constitutional and responsible party, anxious to implement a wide range of social and economic objectives. Side by side with this the party managed to remain on cordial terms with the I.R.A., whose support in the election could also be depended upon.

Helped by its wide-ranging policy, by the progress of the previous five years, by the efficiency of its electoral machine and by the unpopularity of so many of the government's measures, Fianna Fáil made striking gains in the election of 1932, rising from 57 seats to 72, attracting over 160,000 new voters and in the process winning more seats and votes than any party in the history of the Free State. Though de Valera did not have an overall majority he had the support of the Labour party and of some Independents, and thus the way was clear for him to form his first government.

It was a dramatic moment as Civil War victors handed over control of government to their vanquished opponents of less than a decade past, as the men who had fought under arms to prevent the establishment of the Free State now took over its destiny. It was an occasion designed to test the durability and strength of the newly established democratic institutions; the foundations laid by the Cosgrave governments were to prove stronger than many would have expected. The change-over was peaceful, if tense, and the new government inherited a loyal civil service, army and police force.

De Valera's first Cabinet contained few surprises. Included in it were the men who had been with him from the start and who were to continue as members of his Cabinets over the next thirty years—Seán T. O'Kelly, Seán MacEntee, Dr James Ryan, Seán Lemass, P. J. Ruttledge, Thomas Derrig and Frank Aiken. The new government began its life in a welter of popular excitement and this intensified rather than abated over the next few months as the government sought to implement its electoral pledges.[9] Thus political prisoners were released, the Military Tribunal was suspended, the ban on the I.R.A. was lifted and the government began its policy of seeking to appease and win voluntary obedience from the I.R.A. In July the land annuities were withheld and shortly afterwards the events leading to the Economic War were set in train with Britain imposing severe tariffs on Irish imports, thus severely restricting the one export market Irish products, especially agricultural products, had open to them. The government also commenced a task which it was to successfully complete over the next four years—the removal of all elements of subordination to Britain from the Free State Constitution. The first shot in this battle was the introduction of a Bill to abolish the hated oath of Allegiance—a Bill which was to be defeated by the Senate and thus delayed for eighteen months.

These first months of frantic government activity took place against a background of popular excitement which occasionally spilled over in violence. There was, too, growing

Opposition unease about the threat to free speech and danger of reprisals from supporters of Fianna Fáil or the I.R.A., increasing concern among the farmers about the loss of markets and danger to their livelihoods from the Economic War, mounting I.R.A. impatience with the government's failure to act dramatically and decisively about the North, and impatience on the part of the Labour party with the pace of the government's social and economic reforms.

In spite of all this Mr de Valera was in no real danger of losing his Dáil majority and his decision to call a 'snap' election for January 1933 took all parties and many of his own supporters by surprise. It was however to become a familiar and effective tactic in the years ahead. In this extremely bitter campaign Fianna Fáil sought an unequivocal mandate to press ahead with its policies of the previous year. It was assured of this mandate when the party gained a further five seats to give it 77 and an overall majority, its popular vote increasing by over 100,000 to 687,000 to give it the first over-all single-party majority in the history of the Free State. Twice in under a year de Valera had defeated Cosgrave, this time decisively. The long period of Fianna Fáil domination had begun.

Between 1933 and 1936 Fianna Fáil steadily consolidated its position, and by the end of 1936 had a clear ascendancy over the other parties. It continued to dismantle, by strictly constitutional methods, the Free State Constitution. Thus in turn the Oath of Allegiance, appeal to the Privy Council, the Governor-Generalship, the King's name and the Senate were all to disappear from the Constitution. By 1936 all the symbols so obnoxious to Republicans had been deleted and the way was clear for a new Constitution.

The Economic War, the effects of which were to cause frustration and anger among farmers, was eventually to spill over into extensive incidents of violence and the issue was to become a major aspect of the whole Blueshirt campaign. Although failing completely to find the promised alternative markets and unable to prevent considerable economic losses, the government did manage, by the use of tough police and

45

judicial measures, including the Military Tribunal, to break the back of this resistance. It is possible too that the government felt that the Economic War, by damaging the 'rancher' classes, would speed up the destruction of the latter and make easier the return to tillage and the division of big farms among small farmers and landless labourers which was such an important feature of Fianna Fáil policy at this stage.

The government had less initial success in its handling of the Blueshirt movement, and in fact suffered a series of reverses, legal and political, in its early attempts to outlaw the movement. Ultimately it was to be the internal contradictions of the movement and the extravagances of its leader that were to bring about its disintegration.

Throughout this period however the biggest source of worry was to come from the I.R.A. From the start it was obvious that the extra-constitutional military methods of the I.R.A. were totally at variance with the policies and methods of the constitutionally elected government. De Valera hoped at first to win the voluntary obedience of the I.R.A. This proved to be an unrealistic hope and by the end of 1933 the I.R.A.'s freedom of action had been severely circumscribed and its hostility to the government was increasing steadily. By 1934 the break between the two was all but complete. The situation worsened yet further in 1935 and in the following year the I.R.A. was proscribed as an illegal organisation.[10]

By the end of 1936 de Valera had achieved most of his immediately attainable political objectives and in the new calm of Free State politics the way was now clear for him to begin work on the drafting of his new Constitution and the final dismantling of the Treaty settlement of 1922.[11]

The enactment of the 1937 Constitution marked the high point of Fianna Fáil achievement during their first phase in office. Already, after the breathlessness and excitement of the first few years, there was evidence of a change in public temper and even if many of the old animosities were to persist there were indications of a generally calmer and less strident approach all round. This new attitude can be seen in the low-keyed public response to the new Constitution; the

Referendum campaign was characterised more by indiffer-
ence than enthusiasm, and although the Constitution was
enacted by 685,000 votes to 527,000, over 30 per cent of the
electorate did not vote at all. In the general election held on
the same day, for a Dáil which had been reduced from 153
to 138 seats, Fianna Fáil remained the biggest single party
though with fewer first preferences than in 1933. The party
lost its overall majority but could depend on the support of a
number of Independents. And so in August 1937 Mr de
Valera formed his third government and became the last
President of the Executive Council of the Irish Free State.

During all of this time the Economic War had continued,
and although the Coal-Corn Pact of 1935 had eased matters
somewhat, Irish farmers were still suffering heavy losses and
it was becoming increasingly clear that there was little profit
for either country in the continuation of the quarrel. So, on
the initiative of the Irish government, Anglo-Irish talks were
arranged for the early months of 1938. De Valera was to find
the British Prime Minister, Neville Chamberlain, sympathetic
to Irish aspirations and at the end of the negotiations Ireland
had recovered her Treaty ports and the Economic War was
ended on terms favourable to Ireland, but on partition Britain
remained obdurate. The settlement proved highly popular in
Ireland and shortly afterwards in May 1938 when his
majority on an unimportant issue was reduced to one vote
de Valera dissolved the Dáil.

In the June election of 1938 Fianna Fáil fought from a
position of strength and was helped further by the growing
likelihood of world war—thus increasing the need for a strong
and undivided government at home. After a quiet election
campaign Fianna Fáil emerged with its biggest vote ever
(669,000) and 77 seats, and for the only time in the history
of the state a single party won over 50 per cent of the votes
cast.

The life of the Tenth Dáil which lasted for a record five
years and five days was dominated by the shadow and effects
of the Second World War. In this conflict Ireland opted for
a policy of neutrality in which the government had the

support of all the political parties. The sense of shared danger and common cause in the nation's defence effort was to bring about a further diminution in party strife during these years. In addition the fact of war-time censorship and shortages was to curtail political activities and diminish the extent of opposition which Fianna Fáil had to face.

In fact the only real threat to Fianna Fáil during the early years of the war came not from the constitutional parties but from the I.R.A. Even though haunted by some of his past statements and stances de Valera, when he saw that the I.R.A. represented a serious threat to the maintenance of a policy of neutrality, did not hesitate to open an internment camp for I.R.A. activists for the duration of the war. It became in fact the avowed purpose of the government during these years to crush completely its former ally and under de Valera jailed Republicans experienced conditions of greater severity than had been the case even in the aftermath of the Civil War.[12]

The war-time restriction severely curtailed campaigning for the election of June 1943. Fianna Fáil had now been in office continuously for eleven years and it is hardly surprising that some sections of its support were becoming restive. This was particularly true of the small farm support of western areas which was expressing its dissatisfaction with Fianna Fáil through the medium of a new political party—Clann na Talmhan—and of the city workers who were now supporting Labour in substantial numbers for the first time. Fianna Fáil lost 10 seats to give it a total of 67. This left it short of an overall majority but it still had 35 seats more than its nearest rival and so once again with the support of a number of Independents Mr de Valera was elected Taoiseach.

During late 1943 and early 1944 circumstances became more favourable for Fianna Fáil. W. T. Cosgrave retired as leader of Fine Gael; the Labour party split into two hostile factions and the danger of Ireland's involvement in war seemed to grow greater. Mr de Valera once again opted for a 'snap' election and once again the formula worked. After the election of May 1944 Fianna Fáil held 76 of the 138

48

Dáil seats. And not only was Fianna Fáil back with an unassailable majority, but its opponents were in a state of spiritless and chaotic disarray.

Ironically however it was at this point when the party's position was so very secure that Fianna Fáil began to be assailed with troubles on all sides. The rising prices, growing unemployment and continuing shortages and austerities which characterised the post-war years damaged the reputation of the government. There was an increasing number of strikes and a growing intransigence on the part of government to these strikes. It was too an ageing government. De Valera had in 1946 virtually the same Cabinet he had in 1932 and Cabinet ministers who had become accustomed to electoral success had begun to regard themselves as permanent as their civil servants. The drive and enthusiasm of the early years was gone and the ministers had more and more assumed the role and attitudes of the civil servants. And in general the government had about it a tired and jaded appearance, and an almost contemptuous intolerance of those who disagreed with it. In addition there was a whiff of corruption in the air, and while few of the charges made by Opposition spokesmen were substantiated one Parliamentary Secretary was obliged to resign after a public enquiry. More important, perhaps, the very fact that so many allegations and counter-allegations were made was to lessen public confidence in the government.[13]

Fianna Fáil still had one big advantage—the fragmented state of the opposition and its inability to form an alternative government. But with the emergence of Clann na Poblachta as a potentially strong force in 1947 it looked as if this situation might soon change. It was largely to prevent Clann na Poblachta consolidating its gains that de Valera dissolved the Dáil and called an election for February 1948.

Clann na Poblachta did not make the expected impact, but Fianna Fáil itself lost eight seats in an enlarged Dáil (147 seats) and with 68 seats were well short of an overall majority. Encouraged by this, frustrated by the long years in opposition and united in their hostility to Fianna Fáil the various parties did what nobody in Fianna Fáil thought they could or would do—they came together and formed a government. Sixteen years of unbroken Fianna Fáil rule was at an end. The Cabinet was surprised and it would appear not a little resentful of this new situation, and the attitude of the departing ministers was not unlike that of the Cumann na nGaedheal ministers in 1932 who were confident that the new government would soon collapse because of the inexperience and general unsuitability of its members.

The Fianna Fáil party which left office in 1948 was very different from the party which had assumed power sixteen years earlier. It had, it is true, the same leader and virtually the same Cabinet but it was an older Cabinet whose members, not surprisingly, had lost the urgency and drive of the early years. There was little new blood, few new ideas. The radicalism of the early 'thirties was gone, the party was now securely entrenched, its members worn down by their own respectability and regarding itself as the 'natural' governing party. The party had however held on to much of its traditional support and the losses which resulted from the rise of Clann na Talmhan or Clann na Poblachta were more than compensated for by the growing support from the middle-classes and especially from the business interests. Indeed by 1948 many who had looked with horror on the prospect of a Fianna Fáil government twenty years earlier were now active supporters.

(iv) *Fianna Fáil 1948–59*

On the surface Fianna Fáil changed little between 1948 and 1959. During all of that time Mr de Valera was still the unquestioned and unchallengeable leader, his political priorities and values still the same, surrounded by many of the men who had been with him from the foundation of the party in 1926.

The big difference between this period and the 1940s was the fact that now with the persistence of the inter-party arrangement there was a viable alternative government to Fianna Fáil available and with it a new element of electoral competitiveness. This was reflected in the election of 1951 in which, in spite of the collapse of the inter-party government, Fianna Fáil gained only one seat to give it 69 and make it dependent on the support of Independents in forming a government. Mr de Valera did not avail of the opportunity to introduce fresh blood into his Cabinet—it had only two members who had not been ministers in 1948.

This, his seventh administration, was probably Mr de Valera's weakest. It was throughout the three years of its existence a minority government with little real stability. Its lifetime was dominated by the problems of inflation and by a balance of payments crisis—in the solving of which it had no more success than its predecessors had or its successors were to have. It was in every sense a lack-lustre government and in early 1954 it suffered a series of by-election reverses which caused Mr de Valera to dissolve the Dáil.

In the election which followed Fianna Fáil did worse than at any time since 1927, dropping to 65 seats, just fifteen more than a reviving Fine Gael. However the second inter-party government was destined to survive for just over half its allotted time-span before coming to an end in the midst of an economic crisis and a revival of I.R.A. violence. Meanwhile Fianna Fáil had been proving a tough, uncompromising opposition, relentless in its harrying of the government in the Dáil and seeing to its organisation throughout the country —work which was more and more being undertaken by the new generation of younger T.D.s.

In the election of 1957, Fianna Fáil, although it improved its popular vote by less than 20,000 on 1954, won its highest ever total of Dáil seats—78—and Mr de Valera formed his eighth and last administration with the securest of majorities. It was an administration still dominated by the 'old guard'. Seán Lemass, Dr Ryan, Seán MacEntee and Frank Aiken of his first Cabinet were members of this Cabinet also, as were Oscar Traynor, Paddy Smith and Seán Moylan all of whom had been founder members of the party.

The appearance of changelessness was heightened by the presiding figure of Mr de Valera, but the appearance was to some extent deceptive. The elections from 1948 to 1957 had seen a steady influx of new Dáil members as older members died, retired or occasionally lost their seats. This new group, men such as Jack Lynch, Neil Blaney, Charles Haughey, Donogh O'Malley, Kevin Boland and Dr Patrick Hillery, were the first of the post-revolutionary generation to appear in significant numbers and their presence was soon to be felt within the party. Thus though the Cabinet of 1957 was still an 'old guard' Cabinet it had four new members—Jack Lynch, Neil Blaney, Kevin Boland and Michael Moran.

The period after 1948 had seen too the growing authority of Seán Lemass within the party. In effect he had led the party in the Dáil during the two periods of opposition, taken charge of the re-organisation of the party during the second inter-party period and directed the energies of the new T.D.s who were involved in this work—and highly effective work it proved to be. By 1957 he was the established second-in-command and there was little doubt that he would be the unchallenged successor to de Valera, when the 'chief' should choose to retire.[14]

Thus in spite of the appearance of changelessness the Fianna Fáil party was changing during the 1950s. It was changing at local level where older officers were being replaced and new organisational procedures introduced. It was changing in the Dáil where a new, ambitious and sometimes aggressive generation of 'new-style' politicians was impatiently awaiting its turn, and in the process producing a certain amount of inter-generational conflict.[15] But so long as de Valera remained as leader the party appeared much as it always had been and it was not easy for the public to realise the extent to which Fianna Fáil was changing.

Then in 1959, after thirty-three years as leader of Fianna Fáil, Mr de Valera resigned and resigned also as Taoiseach so that he might contest the Presidency, which he did successfully. At this stage he was 77 years of age, his eyesight was failing and he had been talking for some time of retiring. There was no pressure on him to resign; he did so completely of his own accord and both his own resignation and the transfer of power to his successor Seán Lemass were effected without controversy or opposition. It was difficult for many people to think of Fianna Fáil without de Valera. For many, both supporters and opponents, Fianna Fáil was, and would always be, de Valera's party. And in truth he had dominated the party in a way which few leaders of democratic parties can hope to emulate. For the thirty-three years from 1926 to 1957 his leadership was unquestioned and unchallenged. He stamped his personality on the party and during all of this time remained its biggest single electoral asset. Even at times when the popularity of the party was sagging, his personal popularity never did. It had sometimes been claimed that the difference between Fianna Fáil and the other parties was de Valera, and without him Fianna Fáil would be no more successful than the others. The time to test that proposition had arrived.

(v) *The Lemass Years 1959–66*

The appointment of Seán Lemass as Taoiseach brought no immediate or radical changes either in government policy or in the fortunes of Fianna Fáil. He continued with virtually the same Cabinet and within the same policy framework. Within the government however he actively encouraged the younger ministers to innovate and experiment and he impressed his own pragmatic business-like style on the workings of the Cabinet. Though he himself was a member of de Valera's first government his vigorous style and business-like approach was much closer to that of his younger ministers than to his own older colleagues, and his style indeed was to be well suited to the new emphasis on social and economic issues of the late 1950s and early 1960s.

His first major test as party leader came in the general election of 1961. The Fianna Fáil vote dropped and the party was reduced to 70 seats. This was less than an overall majority but with the help of some Independents Lemass secured a stable working majority. This election saw the disappearance of further older members and of the 70 Fianna Fáil T.D.s

53

eleven were new members including George Colley, Brian
Lenihan and P. J. Lalor. Lemass however made no dramatic
changes in his Cabinet (Aiken, MacEntee, Dr Ryan and
Paddy Smith were all in senior positions) but he did con-
tinue to introduce new blood, with Charles Haughey and Dr
P. J. Hillery both becoming Ministers.

By this stage the inter-party alliance of the 1950s had
broken down, with Labour determined to follow an independent strategy, and this was to prove a source of strength
to Fianna Fáil, leaving it the only party of the three capable
of winning sufficient seats to form a stable government. Thus
it was that the main issue in the elections of this decade was
not so much on questions of policy as on the question of
available alternatives to Fianna Fáil. During this decade also
Fianna Fáil retained its organisational superiority over the
other parties. In fact a new professionalism in this field was
becoming evident and the party's need for more money to
finance its operations was driving it into closer and closer
alliance with major business interests. For the most part however this increasingly close identification of the party with
business interests did not seem to be causing the party to
abandon any significant element of its traditional approach.

In the general election of 1965 the exodus of the 'old guard'
continued, some going voluntarily, others being pushed
gently but firmly. By this time Lemass had assumed a position
of dominance in his party which, if not as spectacular as that
of de Valera, was every bit as real, and the Fianna Fáil publicity campaign centred around Lemass's qualities of leadership. The election was to see the votes of all three major
parties rise, Fianna Fáil's from 512,000 to 597,000. The party
won 72 of the 144 seats which gave it in fact a slight working
majority. (The Ceann Comhairle was of the Labour party
and the two Independents were, if anything, pro Fianna Fáil.)

The only survivor of 1932 included in this, Lemass's third
Cabinet, was Frank Aiken. Gone now were Dr Jim Ryan
(retired) and Seán MacEntee (reluctantly but firmly to the
back-benches) and Lemass introduced into his Cabinet George
Colley, Donogh O'Malley, Joseph Brennan and shortly after-

wards Seán Flanagan. Apart from Lemass and Aiken the longest serving member of the Cabinet was now Erskine Childers (appointed first in 1951, and a Parliamentary Secretary since 1944).

Lemass resigned as Taoiseach in November 1966. There was no pressure on him to resign nor were there any indications of failing health or disability. However, it seems that by the middle of 1966 he had decided to make way for a younger man and it may well be, as has been suggested, that the timing of his resignation was 'a political decision, calculated to allow Fianna Fáil to surmount a short-term economic problem and leaving enough time for the new incumbent to establish himself before the next general election'.[16] In any event his resignation faced Fianna Fáil, for the first time in the forty years of the party's existence, with the task of electing a new leader.

In spite of the fact that Lemass had been hinting about retiring for some time the party was unprepared for the contest. At first only two candidates declared themselves, Charles Haughey and George Colley. When it became clear that each of these was unacceptable to sections of the party Neil Blaney, backed by Kevin Boland, entered the contest. However, shortly afterwards a strong movement began in favour of Jack Lynch, largely perhaps because he was seen as the man who could hold all groups together. When it became clear that Lynch would be generally acceptable, Haughey and Blaney withdrew their candidatures but Colley persisted only to be beaten by 51 votes to 19 in the parliamentary party contest.

Thus after seven years as Taoiseach and twenty-one as a Minister, Seán Lemass retired from office. He had been far more than a transitional Prime Minister. Under him the party shifted its emphasis in policy matters; older men were replaced with younger, the party's organisation made still more efficient. This influence was felt at all levels in the party and he stamped the imprint of his vigorous, pragmatic and decisive personality on both the party and the government.

55

(vi) *Jack Lynch 1966–*

During the first three years of Lynch's leadership there was little indication that Fianna Fáil was changing. True the party was more and more in the hands of the younger men, but the generation change had been gradual and within the Cabinet Frank Aiken, and to a lesser extent, Erskine Childers and Michael Hilliard, ensured a sense of continuity. Within a year of taking office Lynch led Fianna Fáil to victory in four by-elections—victories which demonstrated at once the efficiency of the Fianna Fáil organisation and the hitherto unsuspected electoral appeal of the new Taoiseach. After these successes he had what Seán Lemass had failed to get in two general elections—an overall majority.

With a safe Dáil majority Lynch was in a more secure position both within the party and the Dáil, though his position was nowhere near as dominant as that of his predecessor. This was in part an effect of his age, a result too of the presence within the Cabinet of ambitious and strong-minded Ministers and partly also because of his preference for a low-keyed and unassertive style. He made no attempts to change his Cabinet or initiate major policy changes.

Lynch's position within the party was enormously strengthened in the election of 1969. Fianna Fáil faced this election after twelve continuous years in office and at a time when there were indications of an upsurge of support for Labour and a move to the left generally. It was during the campaign that the strength of Fianna Fáil's organisation was really demonstrated, and it was this, combined with the inability of the opposition parties to come together and an extremely successful personal campaign by Lynch, which seemed to turn the tide to Fianna Fáil. It surprised most observers by winning 75 seats and a safe overall majority. After this election the position of Lynch within the party was strengthened and he was being seen as much more than the 'caretaker' Prime Minister, a role which had been forecast by some observers and rivals at the time of his election in 1966.[17]

It is not possible from this distance in time to assess the full effect of the Northern crisis on the fortunes and development of Fianna Fáil. It seems clear now that the first major rioting in Derry and Belfast in 1969 produced serious disagreements within the Cabinet, but in the beginning at least these disagreements did not come into the open. Then came the Arms crisis of 1970, the sudden dismissal of two senior ministers and the resignation of two others. This was merely the beginning of a series of crises which convulsed the party since then—the arrest and trial of Mr Haughey and Mr Blaney on gun-running charges and the subsequent expulsion from the parliamentary party first of Kevin Boland, then of Neil Blaney, formerly two of its strongest and most influential members, the open and bitter exchanges between Kevin Boland and Dr Hillery at the 1971 Ard-Fheis, the founding of Aontacht Éireann and the defections both in parliament and in the country, all against a background of steadily escalating violence in the North. Such a combination of crises would have destroyed most governments and wrecked most parties—but Fianna Fáil, both party and government, survived. It will take at least one general election to discover the extent to which this survival has been real or apparent.

Sources of Support

Fianna Fáil began its life drawing most of its support from the lower-middle classes, from the small rather than the bigger farmer, from the shop-assistant rather than the shop-keeper, from the country rather than from the city and from the west rather than from the east.

Writing in 1933 Warner Moss was able to locate four main sources of Fianna Fáil strength.[18] Fianna Fáil, he claimed, was very popular among the young people—in many areas it might be described as a 'society of youth' and he went on to contrast this with Cumann na nGaedheal which 'by drawing upon local business leaders, priests and prosperous farmers was becoming a party of age and complacency'. Moss went on with remarkable prescience: 'Since the members of Fianna Fáil may modify the programme of the party as they grow older, the desertions will be comparatively few. It is difficult to change one's party allegiance without moving out

57

of the community. Therefore the parties are bound to march on to the grave with their membership.'

The second main source of Fianna Fáil strength as seen by Moss was emotional. He saw Fianna Fáil attracting to the party many people whose intellectual conviction or emotional attitude towards the Treaty split was intensified by the experiences of the Civil War. Also in this category were those who wanted social reform, were not getting it from Cumann na nGaedheal and were yet reluctant to join the Labour party. Then too Fianna Fáil gained from its total identification with the nationalist cause : 'It is fighting a battle centuries old and the propagandists can claim that all opponents of Fianna Fáil are opponents of the Irish cause.' And then too it had the leadership of de Valera, which from the very start was one of the most important factors contributing to the strength of Fianna Fáil.

The third source of Fianna Fáil strength was the adherents it gained from what Moss characterised as 'personal bad relations', in other words, the various sections and individuals antagonised by the policies or actions of the Cumann na nGaedheal government—and as the 'twenties advanced the numbers so alienated would seem to have been on the increase.

The fourth area instanced by Moss may not have been particularly important in the early days, but it was to grow in importance as Fianna Fáil became entrenched in power—'local patronage and favours'. Fianna Fáil, out of office in the 'twenties, had little access to this, but once in power was not slow to consolidate its support by using the limited amount of patronage open to an Irish government.

As the Fianna Fáil party changed and grew older so too did its support. In the course of sixteen years in office it was bound to alienate some sections of its support—and attract other hitherto hostile sections. Thus in the rise of Clann na Talmhan and Clann na Poblachta can be seen manifestations of dissatisfaction among two of the party's most traditional areas of support—the small western farmers and the Republicans. It is probable too that by now the party was no

58

longer the party of youth it had been twenty years earlier and the seeming permanence of the Cabinet blocked off prospects of promotion for younger men. But if it was losing some traditional support, it was gaining elsewhere, and perhaps the biggest single change was in the growing support for Fianna Fáil from big and medium business, particularly perhaps those businesses which had flourished under the protectionist policies of the government. This close association between the party and business was to grow steadily over the next two decades.

But perhaps the most surprising aspect of Fianna Fáil is the extent to which it has held its traditional core of supporters and at the same time made inroads on the support of its opponents, balancing together seemingly incompatible elements. As the Gallup Poll cited earlier demonstrates, Fianna Fáil's support is relatively evenly distributed throughout the community, varying little from section to section, region to region or class to class.

Thus for example on the question of class and party preference the figures were : *

Total	Social Class	FF
%		%
8	AB	37
23	C1	48
14	C2	40
33	DE	43
15	F1	38
7	F2	53
100	all classes	43

*For full tables see Appendix A.

or, collapsing these categories, an even more straightforward picture emerges :

59

Total	Class	FF
%		%
31	Middle	45
48	Working	42
21	Farmers	42

Thus for example even though Fine Gael draws the greater part of its support from the middle classes and farmers, Fianna Fáil has a bigger share of the middle-class vote and an equal share of the farming vote, while at the same time its drawing power is a third as great again as that of the Labour party among working-class voters.

Among the various age groups too Fianna Fáil's support is relatively evenly distributed—with one important exception, it would seem, among younger working-class voters. Over 50 per cent of working-class voters over 55 support Fianna Fáil but in the 21-34 age category only 32 per cent do, while in the intermediate 35-54 category the figure is 39 per cent. The main beneficiary here would seem to be the Labour party, but it is important to add that these figures may not take into account the possible rise of Republican sentiment as a result of the Northern crisis.

*   *   *

Fianna Fáil's greatest strength down through the years has been its ability to contain within the same party diverse and sometimes conflicting groups. By skilful brokerage it has held most of them within the fold, preventing itself from becoming the party of a single group, region or interest. In fact over the years it has consistently represented itself as being more than a 'mere' political party—as being a 'national' movement—and in consequence has assumed itself to be the natural governing group.

No single factor explains the persistent electoral successes of Fianna Fáil since 1932. The early policies of the party— republicanism, social and economic reform, a sort of 'populism'—with the leadership of de Valera and a strong organisational backing swept it into power, but other factors have contributed to its staying so securely there.

It is difficult to overestimate the importance of de Valera's leadership. He commanded the unswerving loyalty of a large section of the electorate in a way which has only been equalled in the Irish experience by Parnell and O'Connell. His reputation and appeal seemed to grow with the years and even at times of comparative unpopularity for Fianna Fáil de Valera's own image remained undiminished. For some people—it is not possible to say how many, but they were far from few—Fianna Fáil was simply de Valera's party and that in itself was sufficient.

But if de Valera provided an element of mystique he had also an extremely shrewd political brain, a sense of timing which rarely let him down and a great ability (in spite of a convoluted prose style) to simplify political issues and get them across to the electorate. He was helped too by the virtual national leadership which was conferred on him as head of a wartime government.

In addition de Valera presided over an extremely efficient political machine—one which had been built up by Seán Lemass and Gerald Boland during the 'twenties, one which was at all times immensely more efficient than anything other parties produced and which was adapted to become yet more professional and efficient in the 1950s and 1960s. It is a fact of Irish politics that Fianna Fáil has always been superior to its rivals in questions of fighting, financing and organising electoral campaigns and this thoroughness, attention to detail, and sometimes ruthlessness, has paid dividends at election after election.

Being so long in office and being regarded as the natural governing party, Fianna Fáil has advantages in the dispensation of patronage, not enjoyed by its opponents. Some sectors are more susceptible than others. A recent study of the Irish Judiciary[19] has documented the extent to which membership of Fianna Fáil is an important factor in promotion to the bench. More than one government minister

61

has stated that in the awarding of public contracts or filling of positions, with 'all other things being equal, preference is given to the supporter of Fianna Fáil'.[20] At another level, Fianna Fáil T.D.s are often in a better position to extract concessions or advantages for their constituents than their opposition counterparts, thus helping them electorally.

In addition to the positive advantages just mentioned Fianna Fáil has been helped throughout its history by the often fragmented state of the opposition and by the chronic inability of the opposition parties to provide a united front. Time after time this factor has worked to Fianna Fáil's advantage and has been as crucial as any other factor just mentioned in contributing to its continued electoral successes.

NOTES

[1]Seán Lemass described Fianna Fáil as being a 'slightly constitutional party'.

[2]This section on Sinn Féin is based largely on P. Pyne, 'The Third Sinn Féin Party' in *Economic and Social Review,* Vol. 1, Nos. 1 and 2.

[3]*Ibid.*

[4]For a full account of the Oath controversy see Lyons, *op. cit,* 491-5.

[5]Pyne, *op. cit.*

[6]*Ibid.*

[7]*Ibid.*

[8]Warner Moss, *Political Parties in the Irish Free State,* 182.

[9]Manning, *The Blueshirts,* ch. 2-4.

[10]For a full account of the I.R.A. in the 1930s see T. P. Coogan, *The I.R.A.* and J. Bowyer Bell, *The Secret Army.*

[11]MacManus, *op. cit.,* essay by V. Grogan.

[12]Coogan, *op. cit.,* Bell, *op. cit.*

[13]See essays in Nowlan and Williams, *op. cit.*

[14]See B. Farrell, *Chairman or Chief?: The Role of Taoiseach in Irish Government,* ch. 5 (Seán Lemass).

[15]*Ibid.,* ch. 6.

[16]*Ibid.,* ch. 5.

[17]*Ibid.,* ch. 6.

[18]Moss, *op. cit.*

[19]For a discussion of political influence in judicial appointments see Paul C. Bartholomew, *The Irish Judiciary.*

[20]Attributed to Donogh O'Malley.

4

The Labour Party

The Labour party is the oldest surviving Irish political party—and also the least successful. It has been in existence since 1912, has contested every general election since the foundation of the state but has never won more than 22 seats or 17 per cent of the popular vote. On only two occasions, or for a total of under six years, has it shared in government and then only as the second party in an inter-party government. It is the only established party which is avowedly socialist and is weaker than any of its counterparts elsewhere in Europe. Indeed for much of its lifetime it has been virtually unrepresented over large parts of the country and until the late 1960s had made little or no impact on those groups from which it might have been expected to have drawn most of its support—the urban workers of Dublin and Cork.

*   *   *

The Labour party had its origins in the trades union movement.[1] In 1892 the Belfast Trades Council organised a local Labour party, which however failed to make any real impact. Two years later the Irish T.U.C. was formed. At first its membership was largely confined to skilled workers and it sought to avoid involvement in the bigger political questions of the day, confining itself mainly to more immediate short-term improvements in the conditions of its own members.

It was not until 1909 when Jim Larkin established the Irish Transport and General Workers' Union (I.T.G.W.U.) that the trades union movement became openly political and radical. Larkin set out to organise both skilled and unskilled workers and in addition his was the first Irish union to adopt a socialist programme including a wide measure of nationalisation.

63

Larkin very quickly began to realise the need for a political as well as an industrial wing and so during 1911 there began to be formed in Dublin and in some provincial towns a series of local Labour parties, some of which had members elected to local government boards. At the same time as this was happening, Larkin and his two Irish Transport and General Workers' Union officials, James Connolly and William O'Brien, sought to win over the Trades Union Congress to the idea of an allied political wing—a Labour party.

Not all within the Trades Union Congress were favourable. Some felt that major political questions should be left to the Parliamentary Party and that the Trades Union Congress should confine itself to its more immediate and specific objectives. Others, especially among the Northern representatives, favoured affiliation with the British Labour party. In the end it was probably the fact that Home Rule seemed to be about to become a fact that made the idea of an Irish-based party seem the most attractive, and the idea was approved.

The new party was founded in Clonmel in 1912, and from the start it saw itself in a restricted and narrow light—it was a trade-unionists' political party, and party members and candidates were to be confined to card-carrying unionists. In one sense this was understandable. The organisers of the new party did not want it to be taken over by existing politicians or subsumed into any existing political group. But the adoption of this policy did narrow very definitely the basis of its appeal and cut off some sections which might have been sympathetic.

The new party also faced a problem on the question of Home Rule. Belfast may have been the most industrialised part of the country, but among many of its industrial workers and trade unionists the call of the Orange Order provided a loyalty that was not easily broken and meant that many were implacably opposed to Home Rule. It was in order to avoid a direct confrontation on this question that the party took no position on Home Rule.

The outbreak of world war in 1914 meant that for the

moment most other issues, including Home Rule and partition, were shelved. The party congress refused to take sides in what was a 'war for the aggrandisement of the capitalist class'. Many of its leaders were in fact strongly anti-British, unlike the Parliamentary Party under Redmond which had encouraged support for the British cause.

Shortly after the outbreak of the war Larkin left Ireland for the U.S. and his place as leader of the Labour movement in Dublin was taken by James Connolly. Under Connolly, who was Commander of the Citizen Army, a section of the Labour movement was involved in the preparation for the Easter Rising. Connolly as Commander of the Citizen Army signed the 1916 Proclamation and led his men into the Rising but neither the Labour party nor the trades unions had any official part in it. However, the effects of the Rising on the Dublin Labour movement were profound—Liberty Hall destroyed, James Connolly executed, some labour leaders who had nationalist sympathies were arrested and deported and meetings were banned.

After a lapse of time, Connolly was succeeded as leader of the Labour movement by Thomas Johnson—English born, a moderate socialist, dedicated and conscientious rather than flamboyant. Under him the party attempted to keep its all-Ireland outlook and organisation intact, but it could only do this by playing down its nationalism and concentrating on social and economic issues which would not divide North from South. Unfortunately for Labour, however, the post-Rising mood was producing a new wave of nationalism which was to sweep Sinn Féin to power, dash forever the hopes of the Parliamentary Party and leave Labour stranded. The fact that at this time the leader of the party was an Englishman was to isolate it even more from the mood of the country.

The post-Rising years saw a very substantial growth in the strength of the Irish Transport and General Workers' Union and by 1923 the movement had 100,000 members. Much of the credit for this lay with William O'Brien and Thomas Farren.[2] The Labour party however was nowhere near as successful in extending its organisation or membership; nevertheless by 1918 the party had established itself in a majority of counties and towns and the party gained considerable publicity and won for itself a central role when it led the successful general strike against the imposition of conscription by the British government.

The 1918 Election

As the Great War drew to its close the likelihood of an election increased. Sinn Féin by this stage had established itself as an important political force with a series of by-election victories behind it, with a national organisation extending to all parts of the country and with an ambition to establish a separatist assembly. The Parliamentary Party for its part was by no means resigned to handing over without a fight and was also preparing for the coming elections. Moreover the election was destined to see a bigger electorate than ever before—it was doubled in all constituencies and trebled in some—in short, a whole generation of new electors had appeared.[3]

In early September, the National Executive of the Labour party met to discuss the forthcoming election. The decision then was that the party should put forward candidates for as many seats as possible and that the party should go forward as an independent political party. Any candidates elected should abstain from the Westminster Parliament 'unless an annual or Special Congress shall decide otherwise'. Shortly after this William O'Brien as Secretary of the Dublin United Trades Council and Labour League invited branches to send delegates to special conferences to select candidates, and in Dublin a decision was taken to contest four seats.

In country areas however there was less enthusiasm, especially in areas of strong Sinn Féin support. In Dublin, too, pressure began to be exerted by Sinn Féin which saw the need for an arrangement with Labour if it was to be successful in a number of seats.

That there was a change of view on the question of electoral participation among Labour leaders became obvious on 1 November at the meeting of the National Executive—

and it seems clear that one factor in bringing about this change was that ordinary supporters were hostile to the idea. Thus at this meeting Thomas Johnson urged that Labour not contest the election, that the election be allowed to demonstrate national unity on the question of self-determination. This was not the view of all delegates—some from the North felt that such a course of action would leave the political field to the Nationalists in the South and to the Unionists in the North. But a majority of the members favoured the proposal and Labour thus decided to leave the way clear for Sinn Féin in the 1918 election.

And so it came to pass that in the most momentous election of twentieth-century Ireland the Labour party was un-represented. This was an election which gave a new electorate its first opportunity of expressing its views, which saw a whole new generation of Irish politicians appear and which swept away a group and an aspiration which had been dominant for the previous 40 years; it was also the election which settled—at least as far as Southern Ireland was con-cerned—the question of separation from Britain. Labour by standing back from all of this put itself outside the dominant debate of the day and allowed a generation of new politicians to establish a foothold which they were not to relinquish.

In spite of the lost opportunity of the 1918 election the Labour movement's sympathies were with Sinn Féin. Given the mood of the country it could not easily have been otherwise, but as a result a barrier was being erected between the Northern and Southern wings of the movement. In addition, even though Labour supported Sinn Féin it had no voice of its own in the Dáil, its leaders had no direct role in the struggle for independence and the movement did not have a voice at the Treaty negotiations. And in addition most of the radical youth, who might have been ready for Labour in 1919, found themselves active and committed members of the Republican movement.

In the election which followed the Treaty the Labour party found itself in a position to contest 18 seats—and won 17. Among those elected were Johnson, T. J. O'Connell,

William Davin, James Everett, Dan Morrissey and Richard Corish. Corish in fact had departed from official party policy and contested the 1921 election successfully.

The party took no part in the Civil War, but the very fact that it entered the Dáil meant that it recognised the constitutionality of the Free State—and earned a certain amount of opposition and displeasure from the Republicans.

In the election immediately after the Civil War Labour put forward 53 candidates and won 14 seats with a popular vote of 130,000. Labour contested this election against a background of bitter internal dissension. The feud between William O'Brien and Jim Larkin for control of the Irish Transport and General Workers' Union which was to blight the fortunes of the Labour movement for the next quarter of a century had begun. In addition to being a struggle for control of the union, the feud had personal and ideological aspects also, O'Brien believing in gradual reformism whereas Larkin was prepared to sanction revolution. The persistence of the quarrel and the bitterness and diffusion of energies it engendered does much to explain the poor showing of Labour in Dublin over these years.[4]

Once in the Dáil the party assumed the role of official opposition and during these early years its performance, and especially that of its leader Thomas Johnson, in focusing attention on socio-economic matters and in examining in a critical and constructive way the numerous pieces of legislation was highly impressive. Dáil participation seemed to bring about a change in emphasis in Labour attitudes. During the years 1916–23 when it was outside of the Dáil the party gave an impression of militancy, passing resolutions at its annual conference, for example, which congratulated the Bolsheviks on their successful revolution and which called for workers' control of industry and public ownership of all land.

Once in parliament however the emphasis changed, and attention was now concentrated on more immediate objectives and on the specific detailed work which legislative activity usually involves. The conservative policies of Cumann na nGaedheal very quickly alienated the Labour party and in turn the government tended to dismiss Labour proposals on such matters as the extension of free education and the nationalisation of transport as utopian. In spite of these differences the two parties did have a good working relationship —and by providing an opposition which was organised, critical and very different from the government, yet which was prepared to work within the constitutional framework, Labour did much to make a reality of parliamentary government during those difficult early years.

In the elections of 1922 and 1923 Labour had not done particularly well in the city of Dublin, winning two seats in 1922 and one in 1923. Nor did the party make much organisational progress in the subsequent years. This was in part due to the fact that the party was still very much the political wing of the trades union movement, which restricted its range of appeal; it was due also to the fact that the Civil War split had left little room for Labour and also to the fact that the return of James Larkin from the United States had led to a bitter struggle for control of the Irish Transport and General Workers' Union—a struggle which resulted in the expulsion of Larkin from the union he had founded, leaving him outside the official Labour movement. Larkin was soon to become a strong critic of the Labour movement, and stood as a Communist candidate in the elections of 1927.

In the June election of 1927 Labour in its election campaign sought to focus attention on the economic ills of the country and charged the government with not facing up to the great social problems. It attacked the government's low wages policy and its utterly inadequate unemployment programme. In addition Labour charged Fianna Fáil with complete ignorance of economic affairs.

In the election Labour had its best result yet, winning 22 seats, and shortly afterwards with the entry of Fianna Fáil to the Dáil, Labour found itself in a pivotal position. The party had earlier declared its willingness to co-operate with de Valera's party—if that party came into the Dáil. Now with Fianna Fáil in, the Cosgrave party was in a minority position. Fianna Fáil agreed to support a coalition government of Labour/National League of which Johnson would be leader—but the no-confidence motion failed on the casting vote of the Ceann Comhairle. It was to be a long time before Labour was so strong again.[5]

In the second election of 1927 the two bigger parties gained at the expense of Labour which dropped to 13 members, and its losses included Johnson, who lost his seat in Dublin County, and William O'Brien. He was succeeded as party leader by T. J. O'Connell of the Irish National Teachers' Organisation.

The entry of Fianna Fáil to the Dáil had serious consequences for Labour. In the June election of 1927 Labour had undoubtedly been helped by Fianna Fáil's abstentionist policy, but once in the Dáil such support was immediately won back by Fianna Fáil. In addition, Labour lost its main constitutional role as the official opposition party.

From 1927–32 Labour found itself frequently at one with Fianna Fáil in its opposition to government policy and in agreement on social and economic reforms. Unfortunately for Labour, however, Fianna Fáil's success in developing an attractive social policy and its ability to balance social and Republican appeals was to pre-empt Labour of many of the options open to left-wing parties in other countries. In short, Labour was seeking to compete with a party which was becoming truly 'populist'. It was not to be an easy task, in spite of the fact that Labour sought in the late twenties to open its membership to all and to get away from being an exclusively trades union party. From now on individual unions were free to join the party as corporate members.

The Norton Years

In the election of 1932 Labour won only seven seats with 98,000 votes. Among those who lost their seats was the party's leader T. J. O'Connell and from now until 1961 the party was to be led by William Norton, the secretary of the Post Office Workers' Union.

Labour and Fianna Fáil may have been saying the same

70

things but it was very clear that Fianna Fáil, led by de Valera, with most of its leading members established figures since 1918, with its policy of social and economic reform, its advocacy of a return to tillage at the expense of the cattle ranchers—and all of this on a solid Republican base—was to leave little scope for Labour to find new supporters. And on top of that the Irish Republican Army with *its* mixture of full blooded intransigent republicanism and radical socialism siphoned off whatever extremist support might have gone Labour's way. Essentially Labour's failure to win any real measure of popular support was due to the fact that it was forced to compete, on very unequal terms, for the same votes as Fianna Fáil.

Labour's opposition to the Cosgrave government was total, and after the 1932 election Labour helped elect de Valera President of the Executive Council and instal the first Fianna Fáil government. During 1932 relations between the new government and the Labour party were cordial. Labour approved of what Fianna Fáil was trying to do on the constitutional front—the removal of the Oath of Allegiance, the abolition of the Governor-Generalship—indeed in short the removal from the Constitution of all elements of subordination to Britain. However, by the end of 1932, Labour like the Irish Republican Army was growing somewhat restive and wanted more radical social and economic reforms. This restlessness never came to a head but the very fact that it existed was one of the factors leading de Valera to call a snap election in the first weeks of 1933.

1932 had seen a very perceptible rise in political temperature with the result that Civil War rivalries intensified, old differences took on a new intensity, and Labour found itself with little hope of breaking through the Sinn Féin barrier. In the 1933 election, a bitter election, the Labour party, short of funds, managed to field only 22 candidates and won 8 seats. Fianna Fáil however increased its representation from 72 to 77 and was now no longer dependent on Labour support. The influence of the Labour party was now greatly lessened.

The appearance of the Blueshirt movement in April 1933 ensured that Labour would still continue to support Fianna Fáil especially if there was a danger of its being defeated or being replaced by the forces of the right. And so as de Valera continued to dismantle the Treaty and fight to eliminate the Blueshirts he could depend on the support of Labour. Not perhaps that it mattered very much to him so long as he had an overall majority, and he could rest assured that so long as the choice lay between Fianna Fáil and Cumann na nGaedheal, or later Fine Gael, Labour would have little option but to support him.

By 1936 however Labour was becoming disillusioned and impatient. Fianna Fáil's social policies ameliorated but did not eliminate the root cause of social ills. Nor were its economic policies sufficiently radical. In short the responsibilities of office were making the government too respectable and resistant to change. Nevertheless so long as the choice was between Fianna Fáil and Fine Gael, Labour's position was predictable and after the indecisive general election of 1937 Labour with 13 seats held the balance of power and kept Fianna Fáil in office. But this support did not extend to the question of the Constitution which de Valera was introducing and in fact Labour threw its support against the enactment of Bunreacht na hÉireann. Nor was de Valera over-anxious to have to depend too long on Labour's support and in 1938, with the successful completion of the Anglo-Irish negotiations behind him, with the Economic War ended and the Treaty ports returned to Ireland, and with the growing likelihood of a major European war, he called a snap election in June. Once more de Valera's sense of timing was shrewd and he got his overall majority, while Labour was reduced to 9 seats and a position of impotence once again.

Meanwhile in 1936 the party had decided to adopt a thoroughgoing Republican socialist policy, partly because it was becoming increasingly difficult to distinguish between Fianna Fáil and Labour—and Labour as the smaller group was suffering most. In its Constitution of that year the objective of the party was stated as the attaining of a

'Workers' Republic'. And the party's programme of that year called for the nationalisation of all basic industries, state control of banking and credit and economic planning.

A few years later these sections of the party's policy were to lead to an exchange with the Catholic hierarchy. The hierarchy informed the party indirectly that it objected to the Constitution's phraseology which 'copied the language of Russia and Mexico'.[6] It also objected to sections of the policy which it was claimed infringed the rights of private property. As a result of this intervention the phrase 'Workers' Republic' was dropped completely and the sections dealing with nationalisation were watered-down. It should be noted that the initiative in seeking these changes and in enlisting episcopal support came from within the Labour movement —from the Irish National Teachers' Organisation.[7]

In the World War which started in 1939 Labour like the other major parties opted for a policy of neutrality. The party decided against entering any war-time coalition government, but as Fianna Fáil had an overall Dáil majority until 1943, this question was really of little more than academic interest. Labour with only 9 Teachtaí Dála, no representation in Dublin, the Larkinite split still unhealed, ineffective national organisation and a watered down, almost apologetic, policy, had reached the nadir of its fortunes. It was little consolation that Fine Gael was, if anything, worse off at this stage and no other group had appeared which looked like shaking off the supremacy of Fianna Fáil.

Then gradually but very noticeably in the early 1940s, the party began to experience a revival in its fortunes. Fianna Fáil had by now been in power for almost a decade and this, plus the wartime restrictions meant that the party was now entering its conservative phase. Moreover wartime shortages and the government's 'stand-still' order on wages, however necessary or inevitable they may have been, were proving irksome and leading to discontent. In addition Labour won the support of the unions by its strong opposition to the Trades Unions Act of 1941 which was eventually declared null in part by the Supreme Court.[8]

73

Labour gained many new supporters during these years. In 1941 Jim Larkin rejoined the party he had helped to found thirty years earlier and the following year was elected to Dublin Corporation as an official Labour candidate. Efforts were made to build up constituency associations and new branches were formed. This impression of progress was confirmed in the local government elections of 1942 when Labour's share of the vote and of council seats rose sharply. Labour membership on county councils rose from 5 per cent to 16 per cent; the party won 100 county council seats as against 37 in 1934; and most impressive of all, the party won the largest number of seats on Dublin Corporation—at a time when the party had no Dublin Dáil representative. Labour mayors were elected in Dublin and Cork. Heartened by this upsurge of popular support and with its organisation and finance better than ever before, Labour faced the 1943 general election with a certain amount of new confidence. The party was able to nominate more candidates than ever before—70.

Relations between the three parties were now in a state of metamorphosis. Fine Gael under W. T. Cosgrave was talking in terms of an all-party government though this evoked nothing positive by way of response from Labour or Fianna Fáil. The hitherto cordial relations between these two parties had now soured considerably—a process which was accelerated sharply by Fianna Fáil's playing on the 'red scare' during the campaign, alleging communist influence within the Labour party.[9]

In the election which followed, Labour for the first time won more than 200,000 votes, winning 17 seats and losing narrowly in half as many more. It was not a major breakthrough but the party did appear to have captured a new sense of vitality and purpose. Once more Fianna Fáil emerged as the largest party but without an overall majority. Labour now found itself in a dilemma. An understanding with Fianna Fáil was no longer possible but support for Fine Gael, because of its 'reactionary' past, was still out of the question. So in the election which followed when de Valera

74

was elected head of government for the fifth successive time, Labour abstained.

Shortly after this however the bitter feud between William O'Brien and Jim Larkin which had been hindering the progress of the party in Dublin since the early 1920s burst into the open once again—this time with such force as to split the Labour party and the whole Labour movement in two.

Larkin had been nominated as a Labour candidate for the 1943 election for the constituency of Dublin North-East. This nomination was not ratified by the Administrative Council of the party (by 8 votes to 7—the 8 who voted against Larkin's candidature were all members of the Irish Transport and General Workers' Union). In an unusual move, the Dublin Executive of the Labour party acting in conjunction with the Labour candidates for Dublin city and county confirmed Larkin's nomination as an official Labour candidate. William Norton supported Larkin, who in spite of a well-organised 'red scare' was one of the 4 Labour Teachtaí Dála elected for Dublin.

The Irish Transport and General Workers' Union members of the Administrative Council, angered at the reversal of their decision by the Dublin Executive, then sought to expel from the party the chairman and secretary of the Dublin Executive (the chairman incidentally being Larkin's son, James Larkin junior, also a T.D.). The motion was defeated and two weeks later the union disaffiliated from the Labour party.

This was followed shortly afterwards by the secession of 5 Labour T.D.s who were members of the Irish Transport and General Workers' Union, and the establishment of a new party—National Labour. Three Irish Transport and General Workers' Union T.D.s—Richard Corish, Patrick Hogan and T. J. Murphy—stayed with the official party.[10]

The establishment of the new party sparked off a bitter and envenomed controversy, with the Irish Transport and General Workers' Union claiming that the Labour party was Communist-dominated and that in Dublin especially the Communists had taken over. The Catholic newspaper, *The Standard*, joined enthusiastically in this crusade which, however baseless the allegations, was, especially in a Catholic and conservative country, to prove extremely damaging to the whole Labour movement.

It was at this stage, with Labour split and in penury, with Fine Gael under a new leader who did not have a Dáil seat and with the danger of Ireland's involvement in the war growing ever greater, that de Valera, for the third time in his career, called a snap election. Once again the formula worked. The Labour vote (both sections) dropped by 69,000 votes and 12 T.D.s were returned (8 official, 4 National Labour). Among those who lost their seats was Jim Larkin. Once again de Valera formed a government.

In 1946–7 there appeared a party which looked as if it might do Labour considerable harm. This was Clann na Poblachta which with its mixture of Republicanism and radical social reform, and a new vigorous image, might well have been expected to erode some of Labour's areas of support.[11]

The 1948 election took place against a background of rising prices, strikes, general unrest and weariness after 16 years of the same government. Labour's split had not healed in 1948 but with the retirement of O'Brien and the death of Larkin much of the personal animosity had disappeared. Labour (two factions) put forward 59 candidates, increased its popular vote by only 10,000 but won 7 new seats to give it a total of 19. Meanwhile Clann na Poblachta of which great things had been expected did win 174,000 votes though getting only 10 seats. Still, Fianna Fáil's majority disappeared completely and the way was open for a non-Fianna Fáil government.

By 1948 Fianna Fáil had been in power for 16 years and whatever earlier sympathy had existed between Labour and Fianna Fáil had by now evaporated completely, with Labour bitterly opposed to a wide range of Fianna Fáil's policies and attitudes. But Labour had been traditionally opposed to Fine Gael, regarding it as highly conservative, though it was reasonable that Labour might co-operate with the other parties, Clann na Poblachta and Clann na Talmhan. After preliminary discussions the desire to get Fianna Fáil out and to form a new government overcame whatever doubts or hesitations there might have been and the Labour leader William Norton became Tánaiste and Minister for Social Welfare in the first inter-party government. Labour also supplied the Ministers for Local Government and Posts and Telegraphs, the latter being filled by J. Everett, National Labour. The effect of working together in the same government was an important factor in helping to heal the split in the Labour party and in 1950 the party was re-united.

Participation in government undoubtedly boosted the morale of the parliamentary Labour party and gave the party leaders first-hand experience of government. But the fact that the dominant party in the coalition was Fine Gael meant that Labour—even if it wanted to—would have had difficulty in pushing through its policies on nationalisation. It is not altogether certain that they in fact saw it as a priority, and furthermore, in the Mother and Child controversy, the Labour members of the Cabinet were on the side of Costello rather than Browne.[12]

In the general election of 1951 Labour lost 3 seats and Fianna Fáil returned with a minority government. Even though Labour had contested the 1951 election as an independent political party, its ties with Fine Gael which had been built up during the previous three years remained strong and in the election of 1954 Labour and Fine Gael worked together for a second inter-party government.

Labour won 19 seats and with Fine Gael's 50 and the support of the smaller groups the second inter-party government was formed. This time Labour with Norton again as Tánaiste and with 4 ministerial posts was in a stronger position than previously. The second inter-party government survived for little more than half its allotted five years. It was not long in power before it was confronted with a serious revival of Irish Republican Army activities and with a new campaign on Northern Ireland including armed raids on

77

customs' posts and police stations. The measures adopted by the government against the Irish Republican Army alienated Seán MacBride who was supporting but not a member of the government. In addition it was faced with a serious economic crisis and early in 1957 MacBride moved a Dáil motion of 'no confidence' in the government. In the election which followed in March 1957, Labour's strength was reduced from 19 to 12 and the party's popular vote dropped by 50,000 to 110,000.

In 1961 William Norton, after almost 30 years as party leader, resigned and was succeeded by Brendan Corish. Under Corish there was a perceptible shift, both in strategy and policy. Norton had been an enthusiastic advocate of the inter-party idea but under Corish an independent go-it-alone strategy was adopted, the long-term aim being the securing of a Labour majority and a Labour government. Thus in the elections of 1961, 1965 and 1969, Labour announced that it would pursue an independent course. In 1961 and 1965 this policy was crowned with a certain—if limited—success, gaining 4 new seats in 1961 and a further 6 in 1965. In 1969, however, after an intensive and at times euphoric campaign, the party failed to sustain this modest rate of progress and dropped back to 18 seats.

In general, however, the 1960s proved to be a decade of growth and development for the Labour party. Relations with the trades union movement improved and in 1965 the Workers' Union of Ireland with 30,000 members became affiliated while soon after, the Irish Transport and General Workers' Union re-affiliated. The party set about re-organising its headquarters and up-dating its organisation generally. It also succeeded in attracting to the party a number of prominent intellectuals such as Dr Conor Cruise O'Brien, Dr David Thornley and Mr Justin Keating, all of whom stood as candidates for the first time and won Dáil seats in 1969. In addition during the 1960s the official policy of the party became much more explicitly socialist than it had been since the scares of the 1940s.

One of the most significant features of Labour's perform-

78

ance in the 1960s was its increased representation and growing strength in the greater Dublin area and a corresponding erosion of support in some traditional areas. See Tables I and II.

Table I—Labour Seats

	1961	1965	1969
Total Seats	15	21	18
Dublin	1	6	10
Rest	14	15	8

Table II—Labour Votes

	1961	1965	1969
Total Votes	136,110	192,740	223,280
Dublin	20,600	55,030	93,440
Rest	115,510	137,710	129,840

In spite however of its more definite commitment to socialism, its increased union support, its strengthened organisation and augmented intellectual resources, and its growth in Dublin, the Labour party has not as yet succeeded in lifting itself out of its third party position and establishing itself as a majority-bent party. In 1922 Labour had 17 seats, in 1971 it had 17. It was still unrepresented in Connacht or the three Ulster counties and had not a single T.D. in the cities of Cork, Waterford or Galway, nor was there any evidence to suggest that a major upsurge of new support was at all likely.

*   *   *

As has been mentioned already, little research has been done to date on the source and nature of the support accorded the political parties and for this reason it is difficult to be precise or comprehensive on the subject. However, a number of observations can be made.

Perhaps the most unusual feature of Labour's electoral record during the greater part of the party's history has been the fact that its support has been predominantly rural. At many stages in its history the party has had no Dáil representative from either Dublin or Cork. In fact over the years the party has had something approaching consistent representation from only the following constituencies: Wexford, Kildare, Wicklow, Laois-Offaly, Limerick, Carlow-Kilkenny, S.W. Cork. It is difficult to see any common patterns here and it is probably accurate to suggest that in a number of these constituencies the Labour T.D. owed his seat as much, if not more, to his personal popularity and record of service as to his allegiance to the Labour party. As a result the Labour party has often given the appearance of being in the nature of a loose coalition of like-minded but independent T.D.s. Even in the 1969 election a number of rural candidates made it very clear that they were far from enthusiastic about the policies and new socialist commitment of the party leaders and placed their campaign emphasis on their own record of service over the years.

The 1969 election, however, seemed to change this aspect of the Labour party turning it for the first time in its history into a Dublin dominated party. In fact its progress was such in Dublin city and county that Labour displaced Fine Gael as the main opposition to Fianna Fáil.

In spite of Labour's traditional failure to win the support of the mass of the working classes it would appear that the bulk of Labour's support is drawn from that quarter. The Gallup Poll conducted in late 1969 and early 1970 showed that Labour derives much of its support from skilled and manual workers—and as might be expected from a party with strong trades union associations, there is a much greater tendency among unionised voters to support Labour than

80

among workers who are not unionised. Among working-class trades unionists 37 per cent voted Labour while among the non-unionised working class the figure was 21 per cent. (The corresponding figures for Fianna Fáil were 38 per cent and 45 per cent.)

In recent times also Labour appears to be gaining considerable support among the new young voters. The Gallup Poll found, for example, that among working-class voters between the ages of 21 and 35 Labour was the most favoured party (37 per cent—Labour; 32 per cent—Fianna Fáil; 17 per cent—Fine Gael). Among middle-class voters in the same age group the figures were Fianna Fáil—47 per cent; Fine Gael—24 per cent; Labour—18 per cent.

*　　　*　　　*

There is no single explanation for Labour's failure to establish itself as a dominant or majority party. That Labour has failed to do this is clear when one looks at its electoral record and its failure to gain representation over large parts of the country. On the other hand the party has shown itself to be durable and has shown an ability to survive where other smaller parties have not.

The most significant single reason for Labour's failure to emerge as a major party is to be found in the fact that constitutional and nationalistic issues dominated political debate and public attention during the early formative decades. The Civil War split provided issues that were sufficiently divisive and lasting to form the basis for a two-party system and in the ensuing debate, Labour, with its emphasis on social and economic issues, could make little impact. Moreover Labour missed the 1918 election, and while it is unlikely that in the highly charged atmosphere Labour would have been very successful, nevertheless a whole new generation of electors were voting for the first time.

Throughout its history Labour has found great difficulty in competing with Fianna Fáil for the support of the working classes. In the 1920s Fianna Fáil with its combination of social reform and Republicanism, with the leadership of de

Valera and with far more certainty of success than Labour, was to prove to be unbeatable. By the middle of the 1930s Labour found that its policies were so close to those of Fianna Fáil that the party sought to move to the left—though without any increase in support. Labour has managed to establish itself as the main rival to Fianna Fáil for this vote—but has never as yet managed to oust Fianna Fáil from its position of dominance.

The occasional 'red scares' and the sometimes pervasive fear of Communism which occasionally manifested itself was calculated to injure Labour in a predominantly Catholic and conservative country. Thus in the 1920s when the distinction between Communism and Socialism was often very blurred, there were frequent warnings against the dangers of Communism, and the frequency of such warnings was undoubtedly certain to damage a party which called itself socialist. Thus for example the Dean of Ossory quoted by Warner Moss in 1927 could say :

> I have learned with regret that some of the leaders of Labour are avowed Socialists. If the Labour cause becomes allied with Socialism, it is doomed to defeat, because Socialism is in conflict with the natural law, the law impressed by God on the heart of man when he created him. It is in conflict with the fundamental principles of Christianity.[13]

In the 1930s this warning became often more shrill and in the 1940s the return of Jim Larkin was to spark off a further series of 'red scares', this time led by the Irish Transport and General Workers' Union and helped by some Fianna Fáil members. Even in the 1969 election there is reason to think that a 'fear of Communism' proved damaging to Labour, especially in rural areas.

The presence of the Irish Republican Army may also have helped to weaken Labour somewhat in that, with its radical policies and its espousal of direct methods, it may have had more appeal than the more staid and unexcitingly pedestrian Labour party.

Emigration too has hit the party over the years. Those who left the country were those most likely to have been disaffected and to have least stake in the country—and consequently those most likely to support the party seeking the greatest degree of change.

It is possible also that Labour suffered from what one writer has called 'Irish rural and small-town petty snobbery'. The effect of this factor is difficult to measure but Professor John Murphy is undoubtedly accurate when he writes that 'the [Labour] party was identified in the public mind entirely with the poorer classes and thus suffered the consequences of Irish rural and small-town petty snobbery. Few professional men, even if they had been actively wooed by the party, would have cared to join Labour. The farmer was not attracted by a party which commanded the allegiance of his labouring men. . . . It has been well said that to belong to the Labour party in the 'thirties and 'forties was neither safe nor respectable'.[14]

There have been other factors too. Labour leadership down through the years, while usually competent, has rarely been inspired. And the party has shown itself very prone to dissipate its energies on bitter and expensive internecine warfare. The quarrels which centred around the personality of Jim Larkin have already been mentioned. There was the party split in the 1940s, and in the 1960s the party has on more than one occasion found itself in a state of near civil war and rent by bitter personality conflicts—and one of the main effects of the Northern crisis on the party was to increase yet further internal divisions and rifts. At the same time, the party's relations with the Social Democratic Labour party, the Northern Ireland Labour party and the British Labour party gave it an influential role in the quest for a peaceful solution.

Overall, however, the eruption of the Northern crisis has made Labour's future uncertain. Had it not intervened, the party might reasonably have been expected to go on making gains among the younger and urban working-class voters, but in the face of the resurgence of nationalism of the early 1970s it is by no means certain that this pattern will continue.

NOTES

[1]See Arthur Mitchell, 'The Irish Labour Party', a series of four articles in the *Irish Times,* March 1967.

[2]For a full account of O'Brien's career see 'William O'Brien 1881-1968' by Arthur Mitchell in *Studies,* Vol. LX (1971), Nos 239-40.

[3]Farrell, *The Founding of Dáil Éireann,* ch. 4.

[4]Larkin, *op. cit.* and Mitchell, *op. cit.*

[5]See Warner Moss, *Political Parties in the Irish Free State.*

[6]Mitchell, *op. cit.*

[7]J. H. Whyte, *Church and State in Modern Ireland 1923-70,* 82-5.

[8]For a full account of the court decision see J. M. Kelly, *Fundamental Rights in the Irish Law and Constitution.*

[9]See *Irish Independent* June 1943 for speeches and election advertisements of Mr MacEntee.

[10]For more on the Labour split see Donal Nevin's essay in Nowlan and Williams, *op cit.*

[11]See ch. 5 below.

[12]For a full account of the Mother and Child controversy and the reaction of the Labour members of the Cabinet see Whyte, *op. cit.,* p. 266.

[13]Cited by Moss, *op. cit.*

[14]John A. Murphy, in Nowlan and Williams, *op. cit.*

5

The Minor Parties

Irish political life has for the most part been dominated by the three political parties which have survived from the early years of the state. This domination has never been total, however, for at every election since 1922 with only three exceptions—1937, 1938 and 1969—representatives of other parties have been returned to the Dáil. On occasion these groups have played a crucial role, either holding the balance of power or, as happened on two occasions, helping to make coalition government possible.

These minor parties have been particularly in evidence during the 1920s and the 1940s. During the 1920s five such parties had representation in the Dáil—parties as varied as Sinn Féin, the National Party, Clann Éireann, the National League and the Farmers Party. This was also the decade of the Independent with as many as 71 standing in the 1923 election (and winning 16 seats), though by the end of the decade this figure was substantially reduced.

That there should have been a proliferation of Independents and minor parties in the early years of the state is not surprising. In the uncertainty and confusion which followed the setting up of the state and the Sinn Féin split, there were many groups and sections which could not easily be absorbed into or accommodated by either of the Sinn Féin factions or by the Labour party—ex-Unionists for example or traditional supporters of the Parliamentary Party. It was obviously going to take some time for the new system to settle down, new loyalties to be founded, policies to emerge and in general for the new parties to develop distinctive personalities. In addition the potential of Proportional Representation as a means of providing representation for minority groups raised somewhat exaggerated hopes among many politicians during these early years.

In the 1930s the system had settled down considerably and elections tended to be straightforward contests between the two major parties. The electorate was asked to choose between a Fianna Fáil or a Fine Gael government—and the polarisation which resulted left little room for minority parties. Thus in the elections of 1937 and 1938 for the first time since the founding of the state no minor party sought or gained representation.

The situation changed radically in the 1940s. Fianna Fáil, having achieved most of its immediately attainable objectives, had settled into its conservative phase and in addition seemed permanently established as the government party. The main opposition party Fine Gael was in a state of steady decline and the Labour party was beset by internal strife. It was hardly surprising then that those who sought to challenge Fianna Fáil should choose to do so, not through the existing and ineffective parties but through the establishment of new parties. Thus during the 1940s a number of new parties appeared—some like Clann na Talmhan and Clann na Poblachta destined to make a considerable impact, others like Córas na Poblachta, Ailtirí na hAiséirighe or Monetary Reform had little or none.

The coalition governments of 1948–51 and 1954–7 provided an opportunity for the successful minor parties to participate in government. These years however saw a steady erosion in their electoral strengths and by 1957 their pivotal position had completely disappeared. From this point on, the number of seats won by minor parties and by Independents dropped at each successive election until in 1969 there was only one T.D. returned who did not belong to any of the three major parties. This decline may well have been due to the ability of the major parties Fianna Fáil and Fine Gael to appear as broadly-based 'catch-all' parties, to the new emphasis on social and economic issues, to the absence of really divisive issues, and to the return of the Labour party to a socialist commitment which allowed it to attract more support from the radical left.

This pattern was disturbed somewhat in the early 1970s by the reverberations of the Northern crisis which led directly to the foundation of Aontacht Éireann and to the expulsion of a number of members of the Fianna Fáil parliamentary party.

Table I

Minor Party T.D.s and Independent T.D.s 1923–69

Election	Minor Party T.D.s	Independents	Total	Dail Seats Total	%
1923	15	17	32	153	24
1927(i)	24	16	40	153	26
1927(ii)	8	13	21	153	13·7
1932	5	12	17	153	11·1
1933	11	9	20	153	13·1
1937	—	8	8	138	5·8
1938	—	7	7	138	5·1
1943	14	8	22	138	16
1944	13	11	24	138	17·4
1948	22	12	34	147	23
1951	8	14	22	147	15
1954	8	5	13	147	9
1957	8	9	17	147	11·5
1961	5	6	11	144	7·6
1965	1	2	3	144	2·1
1969	—	1	1	144	0·69

Down through the years the minor parties have come into being in one or other of the following ways :

i. As a breakaway or splinter group of a major existing party (National Party, Clann Éireann, National Labour, Aontacht Éireann).

87

ii. To represent an economic interest (Farmers Party, Clann na Talmhan).

iii. As an attempt to provide a major alternative to Fianna Fáil or Fine Gael (Clann na Poblachta, National Progressive Democrats).

iv. A combination of ii and iii *supra* (National League, National Centre Party).

v. Extreme nationalist abstentionist (Sinn Féin 1927, 1957).

*   *   *

In all, 14 minor parties have won or held seats in Dáil Éireann over the course of the past fifty years. They are as follows:

i. *The National Party*

This party was quite simply a splinter group of Cumann na nGaedheal T.D.s. The party came into existence as a direct result of the army mutiny of 1924. A group of 9 T.D.s led by the Minister for Industry and Commerce Joseph McGrath were dissatisfied with the government's handling of the crisis and were also to some extent impatient with the progress which was being made towards the attainment of a 32-county Republic.

This party was destined to have a short existence and was essentially a one-issue party. When its demand that the leaders of the abortive mutiny be reinstated was refused by the government in October 1924, the members of the National Party resigned en bloc from the Dáil. This mass resignation precipitated a mini-general election which took place in March 1925. The new party failed to make any impact in these elections and the government party won 7 of the seats, Sinn Féin 2 and the National Party none.

That election marked the end of this party—a party which never seriously looked as if it might become a significant political force.[1]

ii. *Clann Éireann*

This party also resulted from a split in Cumann na nGaedheal. The failure of the Boundary Commission in 1925 to result in the reduction of the size of Northern Ireland or to provide a basis for the ending of partition, caused great disappointment in the Free State generally and in the Dáil it led to the resignation of three T.D.s from Cumann na nGaedheal. This group, led by Professor William Magennis, Professor of Metaphysics in University College, Dublin, formed themselves into a new party called Clann Éireann. Though the policies of this party were for the most part vague and general it did support the abolition of the Oath of Allegiance and grew increasingly sympathetic to the Republican movement and after 1926 to Fianna Fáil.

The party put forward 7 candidates in the June election of 1927—without a single success—and contested no subsequent elections. The party was to find (the hard way) that there was little room in the politics of the 1920s for any group which was not as Republican as Fianna Fáil nor as committed to the Free State as Cumann na nGaedheal. After the entry of Fianna Fáil to the Dáil in 1927 Clann Éireann lost whatever justification it might have had for its existence as a constitutional Republican party. Its leader Professor Magennis was later appointed to the Senate in 1937 and 1938 as one of Mr de Valera's nominees.

iii. *Sinn Féin*

In the twenty-one-year period between 1905 and 1926 there were at least four successive parties bearing the name Sinn Féin. These parties, which correspond to four distinct periods in Irish history, have been designated by Mr Peter Pyne as Monarchial, Nationalist, Republican, and Extremist or Fundamentalist. The Nationalist Sinn Féin of 1917-22 has already been discussed in Chapter 1 and the Third Sinn Féin party (Republican) was dealt with in the chapter on Fianna Fáil. It is the Fourth Sinn Féin party which concerns us here.

By April 1926 the Third Sinn Féin party had disintegrated

into two nearly equal factions, divided on the question of abstention from the Free State Dáil. With the founding of Fianna Fáil, the drift of support away from the abstentionist wing increased and the party which remained after this haemorrhage can be described as the Fourth Sinn Féin party.

According to Peter Pyne, the history of Sinn Féin after 1926 bears out the hypothesis that the split was largely between pragmatists and idealists. After the split the outlook of the party narrowed and from this point on it was less concerned with getting new members, 'seemingly being more concerned with the holding of occasional public rallies and meetings at which numerous resolutions of a doctrinaire Republican nature were passed'.[2]

In the June election of 1927 Sinn Féin with an abstentionist policy won five seats (E. Cork, N. Dublin, Kerry, N. Mayo and Waterford) but lost all five in the September election of that year. From this point on, Sinn Féin ceased to have any real influence, existing merely as a minor organisation on the fringe of Irish politics, growing more extreme, more intransigent, with the passing of time, until eventually it had little more than a shadow existence.

*   *   *

The I.R.A.'s border campaign of the 1950s was to re-activate support and sympathy for the Republican movement and in the general election of 1957 four Sinn Féin Abstentionist T.D.s were elected. Sinn Féin, however, made little real attempt to establish itself as a political party and with the growing affluence of the late 1950s and early 1960s and the decline in interest in the North, the success of this new movement proved shortlived. In the election of 1961 all four seats were lost and the popular vote declined from 65,000 in 1957 to 35,000 in 1961.

Sinn Féin did not become a significant political force again until the late 1960s when it became increasingly interested in social and economic issues. It did not contest the 1969 election and shortly afterwards the Northern crisis was to split the movement, with the 'Officials' still emphasising social and economic issues and the 'Provisionals' spearheading the military campaign against the Stormont government.

iv. *The National League*

This party was founded by Captain Willie Redmond in September 1926. It was described by a contemporary political scientist Warner Moss as being 'a party of malcontents representing nothing fundamental in Irish political divisions'. Moss went on to say that 'apart from destructive criticism of the government its only policy was the proposal that the two contending factions of Sinn Féin led by Cosgrave and de Valera should be retired from the political scene for a time while the country was governed by men who had taken no part in the Civil War'.[3]

In spite of this harsh contemporary judgement, the National League might reasonably have expected to appeal to two not inconsiderable groups—groups moreover who may not have been over-enthusiastic about either of the Sinn Féin alternatives. Redmond as the son of John Redmond might have expected to win over the residual supporters of the Parliamentary Party (and that party had won nearly a quarter of a million votes in the 1918 election) and to have considerable appeal also among many of the British ex-Servicemen who had returned home to a very changed Ireland at the end of the Great War. In addition the party might also have expected to win the support of those disaffected groups within the community who had no constitutional alternative other than Labour and who wished to register a strong protest against aspects of government policy. Chief among these groups were the representatives of the Licensed Vintners who were strenuously and vociferously opposed to the changes being proposed by Kevin O'Higgins, and the representatives of the Town Tenants associations who were also incensed at aspects of government policy.

The National League put forward 30 candidates at the June election of 1927—not enough to form a government but enough to make it a significant force in the next Dáil. In the event the party won eight seats (Cork Boro', Donegal, Dublin

91

South, Galway, Leitrim-Sligo, Louth, Waterford and Wexford) and got 83,000 first preference votes. When the Dáil re-assembled, the National League T.D.s took their places on the opposition benches.

Shortly after this Fianna Fáil entered the Dáil and by so doing altered the balance of power: Cumann na nGaedheal and their supporters were now in a minority. Almost immediately, negotiations began between the National League, Labour and Fianna Fáil, the idea being the setting up of a Labour/National League Coalition kept in power by Fianna Fáil. Such a government, it appears, was to have been led by Thomas Johnson of the Labour party and Redmond was to hold the portfolio of External Affairs. Such an arrangement was unlikely to have been very long-lived or stable but as things turned out the defection of one member of the National League and the celebrated absence of another, Alderman John Jinks of Sligo, meant that the 'no confidence' motion ended in a tie and the casting vote of the Ceann Comhairle saved the government.

The whole abortive episode was damaging to the National League. It was seen by many supporters as a piece of political opportunism on the part of Redmond, especially since his own background and those of his supporters who were former adherents of the Parliamentary Party were so much at variance with the policies and aspirations of the extreme nationalists Fianna Fáil and the working-class Labour party. Such supporters were if anything likely to be far more hostile to Fianna Fáil and Labour than to the moderate constitutionalists in Cumann na nGaedheal. Had Redmond actually succeeded in forming a government, then perhaps the outcome might have been different but as it was, he was left with the worst of both worlds—he didn't get his government and he had lost much of his credibility. In addition the entry of Fianna Fáil to the Dáil had produced a situation in which there was now a credible constitutional alternative to Cumann na nGaedheal. This, combined with the strain of having to fight two general elections in under four months, was to severely tax the resources of the smaller parties and in the

September election of 1927 the National League lost all but two of its seats—those of Redmond in Waterford (where his family had a strong traditional following) and Coburn in Louth. Redmond and Coburn continued as National League T.D.s until 1931 when the party—which had effectively ceased to exist after the September election—was dissolved. Redmond joined Cumann na nGaedheal while Coburn continued as an Independent until he joined Fine Gael in the mid-thirties.

The National League represented an attempt—albeit a weak and ineffectual one—to break out of the Civil War domination of Irish politics in the 1920s and perhaps in the fevered circumstances of that decade it could expect to have only one fate.

v. *The Farmers Party*

In a country as overwhelmingly agricultural as the Free State was in the 1920s, it was not altogether surprising that the only sectional or economic interest group which succeeded in establishing its own political party and winning Dáil representation were the farmers.

The Farmers Union, or as it was more usually known, the Farmers party, contested every election from 1922 to 1932 and was in fact the only minor party to survive the ten years of Cosgrave government. The Farmers party was essentially the political wing of the Farmers Union and throughout the ten years of its lifetime its concern was almost exclusively with the furtherance of the interests as it saw them of the agricultural community. It never sought to widen its scope or extend its horizons beyond this.

The party made its first appearance in the Pact election of 1922 when it won six seats. Its representatives supported the Treaty side during the Civil War. In the election which followed immediately after the Civil War, the Farmers party, almost certainly over-estimating its own strength and over-optimistic about the possibilities of Proportional Representation, put forward 64 candidates (20 more than Labour)—and

won 15 seats. All of these seats were won in rural constituencies, though significantly, none were won in the poorer
and predominantly small farmer regions of Connacht, Kerry
and Monaghan.

During the period 1923-27 the Farmers generally supported
the Cosgrave government and especially its determination to
restore law and order. Cumann na nGaedheal was undoubtedly the party most likely to achieve conditions of
stability and was not unmindful of the importance of the
agricultural community or of its claims. But by 1927 a section
of the party was becoming attracted by the possibilities inherent in Fianna Fáil's protectionist policy, and controversy
on this question increased just before the general election of
June 1927. In the month before the election, the issue
crystallised into whether or not the party should continue as
an independent political party or seek an alliance with another
party. The party leaders Gorey and O'Hanlon favoured
fusion with Cumann na nGaedheal, hoping thereby to make
'the largest party in the state overwhelmingly agricultural'.
Others within the party favoured an alliance with the
National League—an alliance in which both parties would
be of equal status. Finally, after considerable discussion and
not inconsiderable dissension, it was decided that the party
would retain its independence as a political entity but in
general would continue to support the government.

In the election which followed, the party put forward 41
candidates and won 11 seats. With the entry of Fianna Fáil
to the Dáil and the tabling of a 'no confidence' motion in the
government, the Farmers party was solidly behind the government. However, in common with other smaller parties, the
Farmers were adversely affected by the general polarisation
of support for the two main parties which was one of the
immediate consequences of Fianna Fáil's entry to the Dáil
and in the September election of 1927 the party won only
six seats. Once again the Farmers supported Cosgrave who
was now more than ever dependent on their support. This
dependence was highlighted by the appointment of the
Farmers leader M. R. Heffernan as a junior member of the

government (Parliamentary Secretary to the Minister for Posts and Telegraphs).

From now on the alliance with Cumann na nGaedheal became closer, and in the election of 1932 two of the Farmers leaders, Heffernan and Gorey, ran as Cumann na nGaedheal candidates. The party had been in obvious decline since 1927 and in fact after the June election of that year the party's national organisation had ceased to operate and policy was left to local units. This however had been more a symptom than a cause of the decline. The real causes had been the increasing dominance of the two major parties, the general hardening of public opinion which accompanied this and the transfer of allegiance of the party leaders to Cumann na nGaedheal—a transfer which occasioned very little anger within the party itself. Thus by 1932 a significant part of the Farmers party was all but allied to Cumann na nGaedheal and in the election of that year the Farmers party fielded only nine candidates winning four seats (North Cork, West Cork, Limerick and Roscommon).

This was the effective end of the Farmers party—a party which had begun its life reasonably confident in the hope that it might survive as a minor party of real importance. Its contribution in the early years was substantial and in the elections of 1923 and 1927 its popular vote topped the 100,000 mark. However, it was to find this base whittled away by the simplification of issues and alternatives which followed Fianna Fáil's entry to the Dáil and it was to suffer from internal divisions on the questions of Free Trade versus Protection and on questions of its political strategy. It was to suffer also from the fact that its appeal was largely to the better-off farmers and never extended to the poorer farmers in the congested areas whose loyalty was firmly to Fianna Fáil. During its lifetime it was at all times a highly conservative and un-adventurous party and in this it reflected the attitudes and life-style of the rural land-owners from whom it drew the bulk of its support.

The Farmers party was not, unlike the other minor parties of the 1920s, destined to disappear without trace, for the four members elected from it to the Dáil in 1932 were to play a significant part in the foundation of a new party, the National Centre Party, in mid-1932.

vi. *The National Centre Party*

The original Farmers party had lost most of its impetus by the end of the 1920s and in late 1931 tentative moves were being made to replace it with a new party, a Centre party which, while seeking to protect and foster agricultural interests, would have a much broader appeal than had the Farmers party. The initial policy of this new group included such things as the establishment of a Central Bank, a managed currency, salary reductions all round, tariff protection, derating of agricultural land and the reduction of legal fees. It sought also to avoid any involvement in the Civil War controversies of the past decade.

The new organisation, known at this stage as the new Agricultural League, did not contest the 1932 election as a party but a number of people who had been associated with its foundation went forward as Independent candidates with policies broadly similar to those of the Association. Three such candidates, Frank MacDermot, James Dillon and J. F. O'Hanlon, were elected.

In addition to the four Farmers party candidates elected in 1932 there were also 13 Independents, eight of whom came from rural areas. As 1932 advanced and as one controversial issue after another arose, the weakness of their isolated and uncoordinated position became more and more apparent to a number of these Independents, and especially so in the light of the serious consequences the Economic War was having on the livelihood of many farmers.

In September 1932 a meeting was convened by Patrick Belton, formerly a Fianna Fáil T.D., but now an Independent, with a view to organising a new party. Initially nothing more than a farmers' organisation was established under the chairmanship of Frank MacDermot but the following month a convention was held at which a political party to be known

96

as the National Farmers and Ratepayers League was established. Among the main objectives of this new party were included the promotion of agriculture, greater power for the farmers in the shaping of government policy, the ending of the Economic War, the end to Civil War bitterness and the removal of partition by a policy of friendliness towards Northern Ireland. The first leader of the new party was Frank MacDermot. Shortly after this James Dillon joined the party and its name was changed to the National Centre Party.

In the election of 1933 the party fielded 26 candidates, all in rural constituencies and including six outgoing T.D.s. After a stormy and bitter campaign in the course of which a number of Centre Party meetings were disrupted by Fianna Fáil-I.R.A. supporters (the new Army Comrades Association providing protection at some of these meetings), the party succeeded in winning 11 seats (three by the outgoing T.D.s) and 126,000 votes—making it the third biggest of the political parties.[4] Five of these seats (Carlow-Kilkenny, Laois-Offaly, Leitrim-Sligo, Longford-Westmeath and Waterford) were won at the expense of Cumann na nGaedheal and one at the expense of an Independent (Cork East).

In the Dáil the Centre Party sought at first to chart a middle course between the extremes of Fianna Fáil and Cumann na nGaedheal. The fact was, however, that on one of the big issues of the day—the Economic War—the Centre Party and Cumann na nGaedheal were completely at one. More than that, the moderate nationalism of Cosgrave was much more likely to appeal to MacDermot and Dillon with their Parliamentary Party backgrounds than was the more extreme nationalism of de Valera and Fianna Fáil with the result that as 1933 advanced these two parties—Centre Party and Cumann na nGaedheal—were at one on almost all major issues.

Some tentative moves were made in mid-1933 to bring about a merger but MacDermot was not enthusiastic, feeling that such a merger would amount to little more than the absorption of the Centre Party's 11 members in the bigger

97

and older Cumann na nGaedheal. For the moment the talks failed to produce any positive results.

The banning of the Blueshirts by the government in August 1933 in an atmosphere of bitterness and distrust served as nothing had before to bring the opposition groups together. The banning had the effect of convincing the Centre Party leaders of the urgent need for a new united front against Fianna Fáil. Indeed as far as the Centre Party was concerned, the fact that there would be three rather than two groups involved in this merger made all the difference. With O'Duffy as leader and with the participation of the National Guard, the danger of the new party being nothing more than a strengthened and augmented version of Cumann na nGaedheal diminished considerably. Moreover the fact that the three groups were entering the merger on terms of equality and that each leader would nominate an equal number of members to the National Executive seemed to enhance this feeling of parity and give the Centre Party a degree of influence disproportionate to its numerical strength.

As soon as negotiations between the leaders of the three groups had been finalised and arrangements for the new party completed, conventions were called for 8 September 1933. At their convention, just eleven months after its foundation as a political party, the members of the Centre Party decided to merge their party into a new political party—Fine Gael.

Of the 11 Centre Party T.D.s who joined Fine Gael in 1933, Frank MacDermot, one of the party's vice-presidents, resigned from Fine Gael in 1935 and nine of the other 10 sought re-election in 1937—seven with success.

The Centre Party had an existence of just under a year. It sought to be more than a farmers' party; it sought to find the elusive middle ground between Fianna Fáil and Cumann na nGaedheal but it was quickly to learn that such ground was difficult to find and even more difficult to hold during the 1930s and that there was little room in the Irish politics of that decade for those who sought to rise above the maelstrom of Treaty politics. Indeed as the 1930s came to an end the new Fine Gael party was more and more to come to resemble the old Cumann na nGaedheal.[5]

vii. *Clann na Talmhan*

With the absorption of the Centre Party into Fine Gael the agricultural sector was, for the first time since the founding of the state, without direct representation in the Dáil. Farmers continued to be represented within the individual parties with Fine Gael catering more for the bigger farmers of the east and midlands and Fianna Fáil drawing heavily for its support on the smaller farmers, especially in the western areas.

Towards the end of the 1930s, dissatisfaction with the rate of progress under Fianna Fáil and a feeling that the western areas were being neglected began to manifest themselves and eventually this dissatisfaction was translated into political action with the foundation of a new farmers' party, Clann na Talmhan, at Athenry, Co. Galway, in 1938. This inaugural meeting attracted delegates from all parts of the west and the new party dedicated itself to promoting the interests of the smaller farmer, urging government support for land reclamation, the lowering of taxes on farm lands and more intensive afforestation. The founder-leader of this new party was a Galway farmer, Michael Donnellan.

In spite of difficulties caused by the outbreak of war in 1939 the new party continued to organise. In 1940 Donnellan unsuccessfully contested the West Galway by-election but the party had to wait until the general election of 1943 for its first real electoral opportunity. In that election, against a background of shortages and war-time restrictions, Clann na Talmhan won 10 seats. (This figure is frequently given incorrectly as 14 because of a tendency to include Farmer or Independent T.D.s as members of Clann na Talmhan.)

This election had produced an indecisive result and while Fianna Fáil continued in office, it had lost its overall majority and was dependent for its survival on the support of a number of Independents. It was not a situation which appealed to Mr de Valera and when the opportunity presented itself in 1944 he called a sudden election—and regained his overall majority. Clann na Talmhan held its popular vote of the previous year and won nine seats. After this election Michael Donnellan resigned as party leader and was succeeded by another western farmer, Joseph Blowick.

The Clann na Talmhan group quickly adapted to parliamentary life and the members were active during the period 1944-8 in focusing attention on the special problems of the areas they represented. However, the party never saw itself as being more than a sectional and regional interest group and little effort was made to extend the organisation of the party outside the western or southern areas.

In the election of 1948 the party's strength dropped to seven seats, but these seven seats were of crucial importance as far as the formation of the new inter-party government was concerned. Clann na Talmhan was extremely enthusiastic about the whole idea of inter-party government and it readily supported the idea. Two of its leaders, Joseph Blowick and Michael Donnellan, held office.

However, Clann na Talmhan suffered the fate of all the minor parties which took part in the inter-party government. Its representation dropped to six seats in the election of 1951 and to five seats in 1954. It did however take part once again in the second inter-party government, though with less zest than formerly.

From 1957 on its effectiveness greatly decreased and in that election it won only three seats. In 1961 only Donnellan and Blowick remained in the Dáil and by this stage the party as such had ceased to have any real organisation—indeed had ceased to exist as a recognisable party. In 1964 when Michael Donnellan died, his son opted to stand for the Fine Gael interest (and was elected). In the general election of 1965 Joseph Blowick, the last sitting Clann na Talmhan T.D., did not present himself for re-election and with his departure from politics the existence of Clann na Talmhan came to an end.

Clann na Talmhan survived longer and achieved more than most minor parties. Its life as a parliamentary force spanned over 20 years and it took part in each of the two inter-party governments. It never sought to become a major party—indeed it never forgot that it was essentially a party of the small farmer and rural interests, especially of the depressed western areas.

viii. *Clann na Poblachta*

Undoubtedly the most spectacular of all the minor parties in the past fifty years was Clann na Poblachta. It appeared at a time when a vacuum seemed to exist in Irish political life, made an immediate impact and within a year of its foundation looked as if it was about to become a serious rival to Fianna Fáil.

The Clann na Poblachta party was founded in Dublin in 1946 by a small group of Republicans, most of whom had spent the years of World War II interned in the Curragh by the de Valera government. The leader of this group was Mr Seán MacBride, and although he had not himself been interned he was a former Chief-of-Staff of the I.R.A. and as an outstanding lawyer had defended many Republicans in numerous court cases over the previous decade. As the son of the executed 1916 man John MacBride and the famous Maud Gonne he was a nationally known and respected figure.

Many of the first supporters of Clann na Poblachta were former I.R.A. men of the 1930s, who were now prepared to try constitutional politics as a means of achieving their objective of a 32-county Republic. Others were former supporters of Fianna Fáil who had become disillusioned with the tepid Republicanism of that party, and some of whom in fact had earlier and unsuccessfully tried to establish a political party of their own—Córas na Poblachta.

But Clann na Poblachta did not seek to be merely a Republican party—though this of course was its dominant characteristic. It sought also to improve the social and health services and in general to act as an up-dating and modernising influence on Irish life, and attracted to its ranks some, such as Dr Noel Browne and Mr Jack McQuillan, whose emphasis was more on social reform than republicanism.

The foundation of Clann na Poblachta coincided with the period when Fianna Fáil appeared to be at its strongest and

101

most invincible. As far as surface appearance goes this was certainly the case. It had behind it the unbroken years of office; it had a majority of 17 over all other groups in the Dáil; its party machine was immensely superior to that of its rivals; it was untroubled by internal discord or dissent and it had brought the nation safely through the dangers of world war. In addition the Opposition was demoralised and in disarray. Fine Gael in 1946 had 28 seats, was spiritless and apparently without hope of arresting a seemingly inexorable decline. Labour was split and devoting much of its energies to bitter internecine strife. Clann na Talmhan was little more than a sectional interest group and a plethora of Independents merely added further to the confusion. In short, the Opposition was hopelessly fragmented and leaderless.

There were however indications of a growing dissatisfaction with Fianna Fáil and desire for a change—if only some alternative were available. The Presidential election in 1945 had been a symptom of this, when after a campaign of only a few weeks and with virtually no organisational backing, an Independent candidate standing as a Republican, Dr Patrick McCartan, polled over 200,000 votes (against 538,000 for Seán T. Ó Ceallaigh and 335,000 for General Seán MacEoin).

There was too a generational factor. The Dáil in 1946 was an ageing assembly with an average age of 50 and in addition there was a very low turn-over of new members. The most usual method of entry was still participation in the 'Troubles' and the assembly was still dominated by the survivors of that era.[6] The result was that many younger men, born too late to take part in these events, were virtually excluded from the Dáil. Clann na Poblachta, with its stated desire to play down past differences and break old moulds, was likely to make a strong appeal to the frustrated and ambitious young.

There were to be other more immediate occasions on which this growing discontent was to be expressed—though it was extremely difficult to measure its true extent. The rising prices and shortages after the war, the series of lengthy and bitter strikes and the intransigence of the government in the

102

face of these strikes; the run-down and inefficient state of post-war industry and the increasing—though rarely substantiated—rumours of scandal and corruption all combined to create a climate favourable to the emergence of a new party such as Clann na Poblachta seemed to be.

More than any other factor it was this sense of boredom and disillusionment which helps explain the excitement and high expectations surrounding the emergence and early successes of Clann na Poblachta in 1946 and 1947. Then in the Autumn of 1947 Clann na Poblachta won two of three by-elections and MacBride was elected to the Dáil. In order to forestall the possibility of a major drift to the new party and to prevent it having the time to consolidate its growing strength de Valera dissolved the Dáil and fixed the election for February 1948.

Clann na Poblachta approached the election with considerable confidence, nominating in all 90 candidates (11 more than Fine Gael). Most of these candidates had little or no political experience and in some constituencies the organisation of the party was little more than sketchy. In spite of this however the party seemed to be making considerable progress in the early stages of the campaign but over the last few days the Fianna Fáil emphasis on the stability and experience it alone could provide and on the inexperience and dangerous past of many of the Clann na Poblachta candidates did seem to be having an effect and the innate conservatism of the Irish electorate reasserted itself.

In the event Clann na Poblachta did not get the landslide some had been predicting—winning 170,000 votes and 10 seats. For a new party making its first appearance the result was more than respectable, but in the light of the high expectations of the party the result was a shattering disappointment.

However, the presence of Clann na Poblachta had helped destroy Fianna Fáil's overall majority and by a small margin the Clann na Poblachta parliamentary party voted to participate in the inter-party government. The party was in fact to supply the two most controversial members of that Cabinet—

Mr MacBride becoming Minister for External Affairs and Dr Noel Browne Minister for Health.

The presence of Clann na Poblachta in the administration was to be an important factor in deciding the government to declare a 26-county Republic in 1949, and under Mr MacBride a massive all-party anti-partition campaign was launched. The campaign in fact turned out to be a costly failure, and was, if anything, counter-productive, failing to win any significant international support for the Irish cause, working up strong anti-partition feelings in the South without seeking to get to the basic causes of partition, hardening (if that was possible) Unionist attitudes, and by its general futility convincing members of the I.R.A. that constitutional methods would never work. This became an indirect factor in the revival of I.R.A. violence in the mid-1950s.

Dr Browne was at once the most successful member of the government and the cause (or occasion?) of its disintegration. His imaginative and energetic drive against tuberculosis was enormously successful; his part in the Mother and Child controversy brought the dispute with the Hierarchy to a head, led to his dismissal from the Cabinet and the eventual fall of the government in 1951.[7]

The controversy surrounding the Mother and Child episode brought to the surface some of the differences which had been developing within Clann na Poblachta and led to a bitter personal estrangement between Browne and MacBride. Already, before the Mother and Child controversy, one of the party's best-known members, Mr Noel Hartnett, had resigned because he claimed that the party was now bereft of 'any political or social philosophy'. Now Dr Browne was accompanied in his resignation from the party by a number of other members including Mr Jack McQuillan.

The contrast between Clann na Poblachta in 1948 and 1951 was remarkable. The party faced the 1951 election with its high hopes dashed, the party divided and with massive defections. This time it fielded only 26 candidates; its popular vote dropped to 54,000 and it won an ignominious two seats.

This was the effective end of Clann na Poblachta as an important political force.

The efforts between 1951 and 1954 aiming at the revival of Clann na Poblachta as a political force met with no success and in the election of 1954 the party was able to muster only 20 candidates. Its popular vote dropped to 49,000 but it gained a seat to give it a total of three. The Clann agreed to support but not take part in the second inter-party government and it was the withdrawal of this support in 1957 which precipitated the fall of that government.

The election which followed was disastrous for Clann na Poblachta. Its general organisational state was such that it managed to put forward only 12 candidates; its popular vote sank to 20,000 and it lost two of its three seats, including that of MacBride. In spite of by-election attempts in 1958 and 1959 and the general election of 1961, he failed to regain his seat and subsequently retired completely from Irish politics. The party continued to have a single representative in the Dáil up to the 1969 general election—though to all intents and purposes the party had by now ceased to have any real existence and its last surviving T.D., Mr John Tully of Cavan, was essentially an Independent.

Shortly after the election of 1965 the party was formally disbanded and in the election of 1969 Mr Tully stood as an Independent candidate, polled 3,000 votes and lost his seat.

*　　　*　　　*

Clann na Poblachta proved to be a spectacular failure as a political party and a decade after its foundation virtually all traces of it had disappeared. Its failure can be explained by a combination of factors. For a start the fact that the party was in many respects a 'protest' party meant that in the early stages it attracted many disparate elements which were not sufficiently cohesive to prove lasting. Thus many former I.R.A. supporters who had given their allegiance to the new party and were prepared to give constitutional methods a chance were alienated, first, by the party's readiness to join forces with the conservative and un-Republican Fine Gael, and later by the failure of the anti-partition campaign. Likewise with some of the disgruntled supporters of Fianna Fáil who had defected to the Clann in the early days. It would seem that the Clann's performance in office and its alliance with Fine Gael caused many to revert to their former allegiance.

It is possible too that the party's rate of progress was stymied by the decision of Mr de Valera to precipitate the election of 1948, thereby forcing the party into an election for which it was not prepared. And finally, the party was devastated by the Mother and Child episode which brought to the surface differences and discontents which had been growing for some time and were destined to decimate the party.

In the long term however the rise of Clann na Poblachta was to have considerable impact on the development of the Irish party system. It was the appearance of Clann na Poblachta which made the first inter-party government possible, thereby breaking the monopoly of Fianna Fáil's hold on office. More important, the persistence of the inter-party arrangement throughout the 1950s helped polarise Irish politics into two fairly distinct groups, working particularly to the benefit of Fine Gael and helping to end the fragmentation of the earlier years. This perhaps was the most significant consequence of the rise and decline of Clann na Poblachta.

ix. *The National Progressive Democrats*

This socialist party was founded by two prominent former members of Clann na Poblachta, Dr Noel Browne and Mr Jack McQuillan, in the late 1950s. Despite energetic leadership by well-established personalities and despite too a very vigorous role in the Dáil, the new party made little progress. In the general election of 1961 the party only managed to put forward three candidates. Of these both Browne and McQuillan secured re-election but it is probable that their re-election owed as much to their personal following as to the appeal of their party.

The history of the National Progressive Democrats demonstrated the difficulties facing any small or new party attempting to break into the rigid three-party dominance of Irish politics in the 1960s. In 1963 both Browne and McQuillan sought admission to the Labour party, and with their acceptance the life of the lively but miniscule N.P.D. was brought to an end.

x. *Aontacht Éireann*

This party was founded by Mr Kevin Boland in late 1971, and its foundation was an almost direct consequence of the Arms Crisis and split in Fianna Fáil after May 1970. Mr Boland had been a Fianna Fáil Minister from 1957 to 1970 when he resigned in protest against the Taoiseach's dismissal of two of his colleagues, Mr Blaney and Mr Haughey. Mr Boland's disagreement with the policies and actions of the party leadership continued and he was expelled from the parliamentary party of Fianna Fáil. Later, rather than support a vote of confidence in the Lynch government he resigned from the Dáil and set about making arrangements for the foundation of a new 'traditionally Republican' party.

The party made its first appearance in 1971 and seemed to draw its membership largely from dissident elements in Fianna Fáil, and especially from those who were unhappy with the government's handling of the Northern crisis. It has one sitting T.D. who resigned from Fianna Fáil at the foundation of Aontacht Éireann.

MINOR PARTIES—THE IRISH EXPERIENCE 1922–70

Party	Dates	Description	Greatest Dáil Strength	Fate
National Party	1924–5	Breakaway from C. na nG. Republican/ grievance	9	Electoral defeats in by-elections
Clann Éireann	1925–7	Breakaway from C. na nG. Republican/ constitutional	3 (1925)	Electoral defeat

107

Party	Dates	Description	Greatest Dáil Strength	Fate
Sinn Féin (4th)	1926–27	Abstentionist Republican	5 (June 1927)	Electoral defeat
National League	1926–31	Constitutional Moderates/minor interest groups	8 (June 1927)	Electoral defeats followed by merger with C. na nG.
Farmers Party	1922–32	Representative of agricultural interests (especially larger farmers)	15 (1923 –7)	Electoral erosion and merger with C. na nG.
National Centre Party	1932–3	Moderate, constitutional, agriculture-orientated	11 (1933)	Merged to form F.G.
Clann na Talmhan	1938–65	Agriculture and rural interests (especially small farmers)	10 (1943)	Gradual electoral erosion
National Labour	1944–50	Breakaway from Labour	5 (1944)	Rejoined Labour
Clann na Poblachta	1946–66	Republican/Radical	10 (1948)	Internal strife and electoral erosion
Monetary Reform	1943–6	Maverick	1 (1943) (1944)	Change to Independent
Sinn Féin	1957–61	Abstentionist Republican	4 (1957)	Electoral defeat
National Progressive Democrats	1958–63	Socialist	2	Leaders join Labour
Aontacht Éireann	1971	Republican/breakaway Fianna Fáil	1	—
Irish Communist Party	1920s–	Communist Party	1 (June 1927)	

NOTES

[1] For an interesting account of the crisis see an article by Alisdair MacCaba in *Sunday Press* December 1971.

[2] Pyne, *op. cit.*

[3] Moss, *op. cit.*, 170.

[4] See Manning, *The Blueshirts,* on the 1932 election.

[5] See Manning, *op. cit.* ch. 11.

[6] J. H. Whyte, *Dáil Deputies.*

[7] Whyte, *Church and State in Modern Ireland.*

6

Conclusion

The Irish party system began with the new state in 1922
with little continuity between it and the party system of the
preceding regime. The Home Rule party which had been all
but dominant under the old dispensation disappeared completely while Sinn Féin which had successfully subverted the
old regime itself was consumed in the flames of Civil War.
Only the Labour party survived intact from one regime to the
next but it had not been in any sense a major or significant
force between the time of its foundation in 1912 and the
founding of the Free State in 1922.

Once established, the Irish party system proved to be
remarkably stable. The divisions of the Treaty and Civil War
were to prove sufficiently deep and lasting for the two parties
born of this split to survive as major parties long after the
original differences had lost any contemporary relevance. In
addition the patterns of support laid down in those early years
have varied very little in the intervening years. In 1927*
Cumann na nGaedheal won 38 per cent of the total vote; in
1969 Fine Gael won 34 per cent and, with the exception of
the 1940s when it fell as low as 19 per cent on one occasion,
there has been comparatively little variation in Fine Gael's
share of the total vote from election to election. In 1927*
Labour won 9 per cent of the total vote, in 1969 17 per cent,
and its share has always lain within that range. Only Fianna
Fáil has consistently improved on its 1920s performance (34
per cent in 1927*). In 1933, however, it won 49 per cent of
the total vote and it has rarely dropped more than a few
points below that figure since then. Even the smaller parties

*September election.

and Independents which claimed 18 per cent of the 1927* vote have recurred at intervals.

The presence of Proportional Representation has not been accompanied by any governmental instability. The average duration of Irish governments has been over two and a half years and some have served their full term. On all but two occasions there have been stable single-party governments and even the inter-party experiments proved to be stable. This stability has occurred in spite of the frequent presence of smaller parties and fragmentation generally and it has been facilitated largely by the fact that at all times there has been at least one party sufficiently big to be in a position to form either a single-party government with or without minority support (Cumann na nGaedheal in the 1920s and Fianna Fáil subsequently), or to serve as the stable major party in a coalition. It should be noted also that the 'fragmenting' effect of P.R. has been greatly attenuated by the consistent reduction in the number of large-seat constituencies which has been taking place since the 1930s and which has worked to the advantage of the bigger parties.

It is interesting to note that neither of the major parties began as a local or popular movement but that each was established from the top down. In other words, the party organisations were established to enable leaders who had won their position during a revolution to hold that position after the parliamentary machinery had been established. In each case there was an already established leadership structure and a body of support waiting to be mobilised. It may be significant that whereas Cumann na nGaedheal developed around a group already in parliament, Fianna Fáil was an extra-parliamentary organisation. This may explain to some extent the tremendous emphasis placed by Fianna Fáil on matters of organisation from its earliest days.

Unlike many other countries, class-based parties have not been important in the Irish experience—with the exception of the Labour party which, though drawing most of its support from the working classes, has never won for itself any-

*September election.

111

thing like a major share of this vote. This failure of class-based parties to develop has often been attributed to the dominance and persistence of nationalistic, constitutional and Civil War issues in the decades after independence. And yet this is to ignore the fact that during the 1920s the two major parties were remarkably different in the social composition of the support accorded each—Cumann na nGaedheal was essentially a middle-class party drawing its support from the established classes while Fianna Fáil drew its support largely from the lower-middle class and workers. Labour at that time was a heavily working-class party while the Farmers party drew most of its support from the wealthier farmers. It is in the years since then that the difference between the two parties has become less marked with Fianna Fáil winning more and more middle-class support and in the process developing into a highly successful 'catch-all' party and Fine Gael, while still retaining its essential middle-class appearance, seeking less successfully to broaden the base of its support.

The first decade of the state saw the parties develop along different lines and assume distinctive personalities but it may be argued that it was the long period of Fianna Fáil rule which to a large extent fashioned the images of the various parties which have persisted since then—Fianna Fáil as the natural governing party, highly organised and tightly disciplined and whose ideology has been so emptied of content that it can cover all eventualities;[1] Fine Gael as the permanent opposition, negative and conservative and lacking the absolute will to power; Labour, dull, cautious and fractious and chronically incapable of lifting itself out of its third party state. It is in the nature of images that they often continue to cling irrespective of changing realities.

It is not possible to find any easy or ready categorisation for the Irish party system and in fact it would seem that the nature of the system has changed almost from decade to decade. Between 1920 and 1932 the system could be seen as being a multi-party one with two dominant parties. Between 1932 and 1948 it was again multi-party but now with one dominant 'majority-bent' party. From 1948 to 1957 it continued to be a multi-party system but now with two major cohesive groups alternating in power. And since that time it has lost its multi-party character and settled into being a three-party system made up of one dominant 'majority-bent' party, one stable large minority party (with majority aspirations) and one stable small minority party. It is not certain how long this pattern will continue and it is quite possible that one of the repercussions of the Northern crisis will be a return to the fragmentation and multi-partyism of earlier years.

NOTES
[1]See J. Jupp, *Political Parties*, London 1969.

APPENDIX A

Gallup Survey of April 1969

Weighted N=1,580; interviewed N=2,135; owing to fuller sampling of the Dublin area.

The six occupational categories used were as follows:

AB Upper and Middle class; higher and intermediate managers, administrators and proprietors.

C1 Lower-middle class; clerical staff and junior managers, administrators and proprietors.

C2 Skilled manual workers.

DE Unskilled manual workers, labourers, pensioners, etc.

F1 Farmers over 30 acres.

F2 Farmers under 30 acres.

Table 1

Class and party preference

Total	Class	F.F.	F.G.	Labour	Others*
%		%	%	%	%
8	AB	37	37	10	17
23	C1	48	26	15	11
14	C2	40	21	27	12
33	DE	43	14	28	15
15	F1	38	46	2	14
7	F2	53	26	5	16
100%	all classes	43	25	18	14

Table 2

Class and party preference

Total	Class	F.F.	F.G.	Labour	Others*
%		%	%	%	%
31	Middle	45	28	14	13
48	Working	42	16	28	14
21	Farmers	42	40	3	15

*Others includes 'Don't know'.

114

Table 3

Class, party and sex

Total		F.F.	F.G.	Labour	Other
%		%	%	%	%
	Middle class:				
15	Men	48	26	14	12
16	Women	42	32	14	13
	Working class:				
23	Men	40	16	31	13
24	Women	43	16	25	16
	Farmers:				
11	Men	40	40	3	17
10	Women	46	40	2	12
100%					

Table 4

Class, party and age-group

Total		F.F.	F.G.	Labour	Other
%		%	%	%	%
	Middle class:				
11	Age 21–34	47	24	18	11
11	Age 35–54	46	27	12	15
8	Age 55 +	40	37	11	12
	Working class:				
12	Age 21–34	32	17	37	14
18	Age 35–54	39	16	31	14
18	Age 55 +	51	16	19	15
	Farmers:				
5	Age 21–34 (N = 78)	41	38	6	17
10	Age 35–54	40	43	3	15
7	Age 55 +	47	36	1	16
100%					

Table 5

Class, party, and age when education completed

Total		F.F.	F.G.	Lab.	Other
%		%	%	%	%
	Middle class:				
4	Age 14 or less (N=58)	48	19	24	9
9	Age 15–16	49	27	17	7
18	Age 17 or more	43	31	10	16
	Working class:				
27	Age 14 or less	41	15	30	14
15	Age 15–16	41	18	27	13
5	Age 17 or more (N=81)	48	19	17	16
	Farmers:				
10	Age 14 or less	45	35	2	17
7	Age 15–16	45	41	3	10
5	Age 17 or more (N=71)	33	46	3	18
100%					

Table 6

Class, party, and membership of trade unions and farm
organisations

Total		F.F.	F.G.	Lab	Other
%		%	%	%	%
	Middle class:				
7	In a trade union	39	27	23	11
(0·4)	In a farm organisation	*	*	*	*
23	In neither	46	29	12	12
	Working class:				
21	In a trade union	38	12	37	13
(0·5)	In a farm organisation	*	*	*	*
26	In neither	45	19	21	16
	Farmers:				
(0·5)	In a trade union	*	*	*	*
8	In a farm organisation	37	47	1	14
13	In neither	46	35	3	16
100%					

* Numbers in row too small for classification by party to be of use.

Table 7

Class, party, and subjective social class

Total		F.F.	F.G.	Lab.	Other
%		%	%	%	%
	Middle class:				
5	Upper / Upper-middle } (N=85)	47	28	9	15
15	Middle	44	31	12	13
4	Lower-middle (N=68)	54	25	13	8
4	Working (N=61)	40	20	32	8
1	Don't know	*	*	*	*
	Working class:				
1	Upper, upper-middle	*	*	*	*
8	Middle	46	20	24	10
6	Lower-middle (N=100)	47	16	24	13
29	Working	40	14	31	14
4	Don't know	*	*	*	*
2	Farming:				
	Upper, upper-middle	*	*	*	*
11	Middle	41	44	1	14
4	Lower-middle (N=56)	43	32	5	20
3	Working (N=49)	59	16	7	18
1	Don't know	*	*	*	*

100%

Table 8

Class, party and region

Total		F.F.	F.G.	Lab.	Other
%		%	%	%	%
	Middle class:				
11	Dublin	35	30	20	15
6	Rest of Leinster (N=98)	50	34	10	6
7	Munster	50	20	14	16
6	Connacht/Ulster	49	30	9	12
	Working class:				
17	Dublin	37	14	31	18
12	Rest of Leinster	39	19	33	9
12	Munster	50	12	26	12
7	Connacht/Ulster	45	22	14	19
	Farmers:				
(0·3)	Dublin	*	*	*	*
5	Rest of Leinster (N=84)	42	40	0	18
9	Munster	39	46	4	12
7	Connacht/Ulster	47	33	3	17

100%

* Numbers in row too small for classification by party to be of use.

SHORT BIBLIOGRAPHY

Bartholomew, Paul, *The Irish Judiciary,* Dublin 1971.

Bax, Mart., 'Patronage Irish Style; Irish Politicians as Brokers' in *Sociologische Gids* XVII, 3 (1970).

Bell, J. Bowyer, *The Secret Army,* London 1970.

Blanchard, Jean, *The Church in Contemporary Ireland,* Dublin 1963.

Blanschard, Paul, *The Irish and Catholic Power,* London 1954.

Busteed, M. A. and Mason, H., 'Irish Labour in the 1969 Election', *Political Studies* XVIII, 3 (1970).

Chubb, Basil, 'The Independent Member in Ireland' *Political Studies,* No. 2.

Chubb, Basil, 'The Republic of Ireland' in S. Henig and J. Pindar ed. *European Political Parties,* London 1969.

Chubb, Basil, *The Government and Politics of Ireland,* Oxford 1970.

Coogan, T. P., *Ireland Since the Rising,* London 1966.

Coogan, T. P., *The I.R.A.,* London 1970.

Farrell, Brian, 'Labour and the Irish political party system; a suggested approach to analysis' *Economic and Social Review* I, 4.

Farrell, Brian, 'Dáil Deputies; the 1969 Generation' *Economic and Social Review* 2, 3.

Farrell, Brian, *Chairman or Chief? : The Role of Taoiseach in Irish Government,* Dublin 1971.

Farrell, Brian, *The Founding of Dáil Éireann,* Dublin 1971.

Fianna Fáil, *The Story of Fianna Fáil; First phase,* Dublin 1960.

Garvin, T., 'Continuity and Change in Irish Electoral Politics, *Economic and Social Review,* March 1972.

Hancock, W. K., *Survey of British Commonwealth Affairs,* Vol. 1., London 1937.

Laffin, Michael, 'Sinn Féin 1916-21', *Capuchin Annual* 1970.

Larkin, Emmet, *James Larkin, Irish Labour Leader,* 1965.

Longford, Earl of and O'Neill, T. P., *Eamon de Valera,* Dublin 1970.

Lyons, F. S. L., *Ireland Since the Famine,* London 1971.

Lyons, F. S. L., *The Irish Parliamentary Party,* London 1951.

McCracken, J. L., *Representative Government in Ireland. A study of Dáil Éireann 1919-48,* London 1953.

Mansergh, Nicholas, *The Irish Free State; its Government and Politics,* London 1934.

MacManus, Francis, *The Years of the Great Test,* Cork 1967.

Manning, Maurice, *The Blueshirts,* Dublin 1971.

Moss, Warner, *Political Parties in the Irish Free State,* New York 1934.

Nowlan, K. and Williams, D., *Ireland in the War Years and after,* Dublin 1969.

O'Brien, Conor Cruise ed., *Conor Cruise O'Brien introduces Ireland,* London 1969.

O'Connor Lysaght, D. R., *The Irish Republic,* Cork 1970.

O'Leary, Cornelius, *The Irish Republic and its experiment with Proportional Representation,* Notre Dame 1961.

O'Sullivan, Donal, *The Irish Free State and its Senate,* London 1940.

Pyne, Peter, 'The Third Sinn Féin Party 1923-26', *Economic and Social Review* 1, 1 and 2.

Rumpf, Erhard, *Nationalismus und Sozialismus in Irland,* Mannheim 1969.

Sacks, Paul, 'Bailiwicks, Locality and Religion; Three elements in an Irish Dáil Constituency Election', *Economic and Social Review* 1, 4.

Whyte, J. H., *Dáil Deputies,* Dublin 1966.

Whyte, J. H., *Church and State in Modern Ireland 1923-70,* Dublin 1971.